Pain and Suffering

Pain is felt by everyone, yet understanding its nature is fragmented across myriad modes of thought. In this compact, yet thoroughly integrative account uniting medical science, psychology, and the humanities Ronald Schleifer offers a deep and complex understanding, along with possible strategies of dealing with pain in its most overwhelming forms. A perfect addition to many courses in medicine, healthcare, counseling psychology, and social work.

Ronald Schleifer is George Lynn Cross Research Professor in the Department of English at the University of Oklahoma, where he is also Adjunct Professor in Medicine. His most recent books include *Intangible Materialism: The Body, Scientific Knowledge, and the Power of Language* (2009), *Modernism and Popular Music* (2011), and *The Chief Concern of Medicine: The Integration of the Medical Humanities and Narrative Knowledge into Medical Practices*, co-authored with Dr. Jerry Vannatta (2013). He has served as editor of the scholarly journals *Genre: Forms of Discourse and Culture* and *Configurations: A Journal of Literature, Science, and Technology*.

The Routledge Series Integrating Science and Culture

Editor: Lennard J. Davis, University of Illinois at Chicago

The Routledge Series Integrating Science and Culture aims to reunite the major discourses of science and the humanities that parted ways about 150 years ago. Each book picks an important topic that can best be understood by a synthesis of the best science and the best social and cultural analysis. In an age when more and more major political and life decisions involve complex understandings of science, medicine, and technology, we need to have a bioculturally sophisticate citizenry who can weigh in on these important issues. To that end these books aim to reach a wide swathe of people, presenting the information in readable, illustrated, succinct editions that are designed for classroom and scholarly use as well as for public consumption.

Available

Autism by Stuart Murray

Depression: Integrating Science, Culture, and Humanities by Bradley Lewis

Sex/Gender: Biology in a Social World by Anne Fausto-Sterling

Titles of Related Interest

Creating Sanctuary: Toward the Evolution of Sane Societies, Revised Edition by Sandra L. Bloom

Pain and Suffering

Ronald Schleifer

Routledge
Taylor & Francis Group

NEW YORK AND LONDON

First published 2014
by Routledge
711 Third Avenue, New York, NY 10017

and by Routledge
2 Park Square, Milton Park, Abingdon, Oxon, OX14 4RN

Routledge is an imprint of the Taylor & Francis Group, an informa business

© 2014 Taylor & Francis

Library of Congress Cataloging in Publication Data
  Schleifer, Ronald.
  Pain and suffering / by Ronald Schleifer.
    pages cm. — (The Routledge series integrating science and culture)
    Summary: "Pain is felt by everyone, yet understanding its nature is
    fragmented across myriad modes of thought. In this compact, yet thoroughly
    integrative account uniting medical science, psychology, and the humanities
    Ronald Schleifer offers a deep and complex understanding along with
    possible strategies of dealing with pain in its most overwhelming forms.
    A perfect addition to many courses in medicine, healthcare, counseling
    psychology, and social work" — Provided by publisher.
    Includes bibliographical references and index.
    1. Pain. 2. Suffering. I. Title.
    RB127.S347 2014
    616′.0472–dc23
    2013030565

ISBN: 978–0–415–84326–3 (hbk)
ISBN: 978–0–415–84327–0 (pbk)
ISBN: 978–0–203–75734–5 (ebk)

Typeset in Adobe Caslon and Copperplate Gothic
by Florence Production Ltd, Stoodleigh, Devon, UK

Printed in Great Britain by TJ International Ltd, Padstow, Cornwall

CONTENTS

SERIES FOREWORD

The Routledge Series Integrating Science and Culture aims to restore connections between the sciences and the humanities, connections that were severed over 150 years ago. This mutual exclusion was done in the name of expertise values and morality in the world of humanism. In some sense, each side was seen as the societal enemy of the other. From the humanists' perspective, scientists threatened to make the world a colder, more efficient place lacking in feelings and values. From the scientists' viewpoint, humanists were interfering with progress by injecting bleeding hearts and unreasonable fears into an essentially rational process.

But the reality is that now, in the twenty-first century, it is getting harder and harder for humanists to comment on civic and social matters without knowing something about science, medicine, and technology. Suddenly there is a need to understand stem cells, brain scans, DNA technologies, organ transplants, ecological outcomes, and the like in order to be a knowledgeable citizen, legislator, or scholar. Likewise, scientists routinely include the ethical, social, cultural, and legal in their research protocols and scientific articles. The divide between the "two cultures" described by C. P. Snow in the 1950s is less and less possible in the twenty-first century. On the ground, humanists and scientists are again in need of each other.

To that end, the books in this series will focus on the cultural side of science and the scientific side of culture. David Morris and I have coined the term "biocultural" to indicate this new realm of study and critique. Ronald Schleifer's *Pain and Suffering* is a perfect addition to *The Routledge Series Integrating Science and Culture*. Pain and suffering seem to be terms and conditions that have an immediate and understandable connection with medicine. Indeed when we have extended physical pain we take that as a sign that we need to see a doctor. When we have extended emotional pain we seek the services of a therapist or psychiatrist. Suffering, on the other hand, while having a medical component is broad enough to extend to the existential, political, and philosophical realms. So we might think that purely physical pain is something we don't need to understand in a cultural sense. But what Schleifer does so well is to help us understand that pain along with suffering is a cultural phenomenon as much as it is a physical one. Drawing such a link is important for the general biocultural project because something like pain seems at the outset to be something quite as far from culture and interpretation as anything could be. Pain seems like a bare, brutal fact, as sure as death and taxes. If something with the solidity and "thereness" of pain could be open to a biocultural interpretation and understanding, then there really isn't anything that couldn't be. In this sense, we could say that pain is the limit case for arguing that a biocultural explanation of phenomena is not only valid but also necessary. It is the accomplishment of Ronald Schleifer's book to have easily and seamlessly made and proven that argument.

Lennard J. Davis
Series Editor

PREFACE AND ACKNOWLEDGMENTS

The purpose of this book is to offer to students, healthcare workers, the general public, and those who labor with pain in their lives a working sense of the latest understanding of the nature and phenomenon of human pain to the end of comprehension and action in relation to that pain. As I note throughout this book, pain is a ubiquitous part of human experience—many assert that it is one of the defining features of human life altogether—and a clearer understanding of how it works and what it means has the potential to make the lives of those in pain and of those who share their lives with people in pain less narrow, more fulfilling, and simply more bearable. That is my great hope for this book. To this end, I have examined closely the work of healthcare workers engaged with patients in pain, scientists, social scientists, philosophers, artists who study and represent the phenomena of human pain, and the moving and sometimes harrowing narratives of those who suffer the long-term affliction and distress of pain. I end the book with a chapter that attempts to explicitly articulate strategies of care for pain that can be taken up by healthcare workers, companions, and those who suffer pain themselves.

As I note early on in the text, I come to my engagement with pain from work in the medical humanities. My own formal training is in language and literature: I have focused my work on twentieth-century literary studies, semiotics, cultural studies with an emphasis on discourse theory and music, and, during last decade, I have been engaged in the medical humanities. As I note in Appendix I to this book, I have come to believe that work on the humanities and cultural studies can and should be as systematically rigorous as work in the physical and social sciences; and that such work offers possibilities of *effective action* in our thinking and behavior. To that end, as I suggest throughout this book, the examination of the nature and phenomenon of human pain can and should lead to particular engagements that can lead to its understanding and, to some degree, its alleviation.

In this endeavor, I have been helped by many. First of all I want to acknowledge and thank Lennard Davis, a long-time friend and colleague, who encouraged me to take up this project in the first place. Lenny's enthusiasm for making intellectual knowledge in the humanities and cultural studies work in the world to enrich understanding and experience—to enrich our lives altogether—is an inspiration to many pursuing practical results from intellectual labor. In addition, the practical and timely aid of Steven Rutter and Margaret Moore at Routledge and Charlotte Hiorns at Florence Production Ltd has made this project run more smoothly than I could have imagined when I began. Among other things, they found a number of remarkable readers from a variety of disciplines whose comments on an early version of this book have greatly benefited my work. I also want to thank the Office of the Vice President for Research at the University of Oklahoma and the Vice President himself, Kelvin Droegemeier, for support on this and other projects I pursue. In this project that support took the form of the diligent and thoughtful work of Lauren Brentnell, my research assistant, who undertook chores large and small in helping me complete my work on this book. Throughout, she has offered thoughtful and useful advice that has improved the shape and accessibility of my work. Many others—my friend and co-author, Dr. Jerry Vannatta, David Levy, Amanda Rook, Elyon Wall-Ellis, Jen Tucker, Anne Jacobs, Jen Crawford, Russell Reising, my brother Robert Schleifer, my former student and now co-teacher Sarah Swenson, my sister-in-law, Edie Mergler, Angus McCamant, and countless friends, but also strangers at conferences, in airplanes and coffee shops, who were willing to discuss this topic, which is of interest to us all—have helped clarify and sharpen my work. And a special thank you to the reviewers:

John Coulehan	SUNY Stonybrook
Robert Markley	University of Illinois, Urbana-Champaign
Theresa Scheid	University of North Carolina, Charlotte
Chuck Peek	University of Florida
David Morris	University of Virginia/Semester at Sea

Many who study and engage with human pain note that while pain is *absolutely real* to those who suffer it, it is easily seen to be *unreal* and easily dismissed by those who listen to suffering people describe their condition, and in working on this book engagements with students— pre-med, medical students, young people studying the arts and humanities, physicians and healthcare workers, who are themselves lifelong students—have helped me to articulate strategies for making pain real for those outside its sufferings. In this endeavor, I hope this book is, at least in small ways, successful. Most of all I want to acknowledge and thank my wife, Nancy Mergler, who has put up with times of listening to all kinds of babble, to shocking narratives and examples that have haunted me, to my strange excitement of engaging a topic that arouses strong distress and anxiety (and, I like to think, hope as well), with patience, goodwill, and enacted antidotes to the sadness, dismay, and even revulsion that pain and suffering provoke. Nancy, along with our sons Cyrus and Benjamin, and many friends, named and unnamed here, constantly remind me that even the most unbearable pain can, and often does, exist within communities of affection, care, and loving kindnesses.

A Note on the Images

The images presented throughout this book—associated with chapter titles and the book's cover image—are used courtesy of History of Science Collections, University of Oklahoma Libraries. Specifically, they are taken from first editions of great sixteenth-century treatises studying the human body for medical purposes: *De humani corporis fabrica* (On the fabric of the human body, Basel 1543) by Andreas Vesalius, who stares out at us at the beginning of Chapter 7 as he treats the human hand: many scholars believe this treatise was illustrated by Titian's pupil Jan Stephen van Calcar; *De dissectione partium corporis humani* (On the dissection of the parts of the human body, Paris 1545) by Charles

Estienne, with well-drawn woodcuts; and a final image, chosen to illustrate torture at the title of Chapter 6, from *Physicas* (Physic, Strassburg, 1533) by the medieval polymath, Hildegard of Bingen, who lived a monastic life in a convent in the twelfth century: in 1533 an illustrated version of her book was issued in Strassburg, and on October 7 2012, Pope Benedict XVI named her a Doctor of the Church. All of these images illustrate the great Renaissance and Enlightenment rethinking of human body in general and pain more specifically that is mentioned throughout this book. The cover image appears in Estienne, p. 163 (it is also part of the montage of suffering for Chapter 5); the image for Chapter 1 is a "representation" of pain from Estienne, p. 59; for Chapter 2 is a rendition of what came to be called the "spinothalamic tract" from Vesalius, p. 319; for Chapter 3 a detail from an image, chosen to illustrate chronic pain, from Estienne, p. 285; for Chapter 4, instruments of surgery from Vesalius, p. 200; for Chapter 5, a montage of details of faces from anatomical drawings, Estienne, pp. 163, 279, 166, 165, 168, 285 and Vesalius, p. 170; for Chapter 6, Hildegard, second frontispiece; for Chapter 7, Vesalius frontispiece. The illustration of double-reed instruments in Chapter 7 is taken from the *Encyclopedia Britannica* (American reprint), 9th edition, vol. 17 (Philadelphia, 1884), p. 725. I also want to thank the Curator of the History of Science Collection, Professor Kerry Magruder, for his careful advice and unstinting time in organizing the images for this book.

INTRODUCTION

1

THE FACT AND EXPERIENCE OF PAIN: SCIENCE AND THE HUMANITIES

Anything beyond the most commonplace acute pain is a complex perceptual experience taking place not strictly within the individual nervous system but also within the open-ended, social field of human thought and action. Pain, we are slowly beginning to recognize, is far more than merely a medical issue. It exists within us only as it wraps itself up, for better or worse, in meaning.

—David Morris, *The Culture of Pain* (1991: 269)

Pain and Suffering

Pain and suffering have been and remain essential elements of human life, just as joy, community, and happiness are also essential elements of human life. In recent times, however, in the United States and western countries, we have become more and more reluctant to acknowledge and face these aspects of our private and social lives. Television commercials proclaim to us that pain is unnecessary and easily banished from our experience; and it is widely assumed that pain and suffering can lead to no positive outcomes. This situation both grows out of and reinforces the sense that *pain*, a physiological condition that seems exclusively related to and affects the body, is different in quality and meaning from

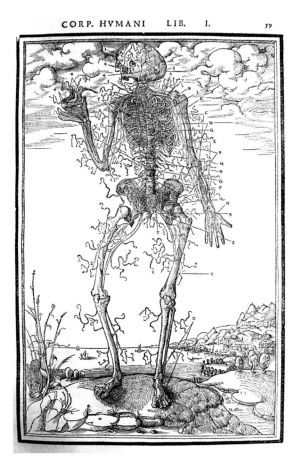

CORP. HVMANI LIB. I. 59

Figure 1.1 The Fact and Experience of Pain

suffering, a psychological or spiritual condition that is the meaning and significance of the experience of pain as it affects the individual. That is, the separation of pain and suffering participates in the separation of science and culture, which the Routledge Series aims to help us reconsider in our classrooms and in our thinking. This separation is clearly depicted in a short story by Ernest Hemingway, "Indian Camp", where a doctor performs a caesarian section on a woman while his young son watches:

> "Oh, Daddy, can't you give her something to make her stop screaming?" asked Nick.

"No. I haven't any anaesthetic," his father said. "But her screams are not important. I don't hear them because they are not important."

The husband in the upper bunk rolled over against the wall.

(1970: 17)

I bring up this small scene here at the beginning of this book because the practical issue of a study of pain and suffering is the question of how healthcare workers, who encounter pain and suffering on a daily basis, understand and respond to these human experiences. But this study is also important in examining how the rest of us understand and respond to these experiences in our own lives and those with whom we share our lives. That is, it is clear that pain *is* important: as Robinson Jeffers says in one of his poems, "happiness is important, but pain *gives* importance" (1955: 244). The importance of pain—how it works, what it means, its place within the wider experiences of life—is the focus of this book. The separation of pain and suffering that the physician in Hemingway's story expresses sets forth the nature of pain as it is usually understood. Pain is clearly a *fact*, an *event* that happens at a particular moment. But almost all the people who study human pain— physiologists, anesthesiologists, neurologists, philosophers, historians, aestheticians, etc.—and *all* people who find themselves in pain understand that whatever else pain is, it is also always a powerful human *experience*. Pain, most people who study it agree, both is a fact and/or an event, a phenomenon that can be studied by the natural sciences; and it is also a deeply human experience, studied by the human sciences. These two conceptions of pain, as we shall see throughout this book, are captured by the fact that pain is understood, respectively and often simultaneously, as a *sensation* and as a *perception*.

The commonplace separation of pain and suffering participates in the separation of science and culture, which the Routledge Series aims to help us reconsider. This separation is apparently depicted—but also oddly erased—in an account of a bizarre and curious incident that occurred early in Dr. Frank Vertosick's medical career. Vertosick describes one patient who had an emergency open-heart surgery when he hemorrhaged in his recovery room two days after his initial surgery.

He had become unconscious, and surgeons opened his chest. After his aorta was repaired without any anesthetic, the patient received oxygen to his brain and woke, only to see his exposed heart, which was "twisting and splashing within his open chest," and he began screaming in pain at the top of his lungs. An anesthesiologist joined the team—by this time the room was covered in blood—and administered a paralytic drug so that the patient stopped moving, and additional drugs that returned him to unconsciousness. These additional drugs included a "dissociative anesthesia," the anesthesiologist said, so the patient wouldn't remember the horror he had gone through. The surgeons then repaired the patient's heart and chest without further incident. Just before he was discharged, Dr. Vertosick asked him how he enjoyed his stay in the hospital. He replied:

> "Oh, great. A very nice place. In fact, this whole experience has been better than I could have imagined. Except for that nasty thing in the ICU."
> "What nasty thing?"
> "The low-salt chicken soup. Who ever heard of low-salt chicken soup? I don't think I could tolerate that stuff again."
> (2000: 192–97)

This is a strange and provocative narrative about the nature of pain that suggests, bizarrely as I said, that somehow pain is no longer pain when it is not a remembered experience. That is, this story seems to contradict that of Hemingway, where the physician dissociates the seeming meaningless *fact* of pain and the *felt meaning* of suffering. Here, the forgetfulness of suffering renders the patient's pain seemingly—or perhaps in fact—non-existent.

For this reason, it raises all kinds of questions. Among other things, it raises the question whether the physiological facts/events that take place even when we are rendered unconscious by anesthetics can be thought of as "pain" even though they are unremembered. But more starkly, this narrative, and the phenomenon of pain more generally, raise questions concerning the integration of the sciences and the humanities that is the focus of the Routledge Series. As fact or event (which is to say, as conceived in relation to a stimulus and response), pain is subject to scientific analysis; yet because it is necessarily conscious, *necessarily experienced*—and in this bizarre case a necessarily *remembered* experience —it is intimately tied up with any notion we might have of self or personhood, with the meanings and values that the humanities and cultural studies engage.

I also bring up this strange scene here at the beginning of this book because the practical issue of a study of pain and suffering is the question of how healthcare workers, who encounter pain and suffering on a daily basis, understand and respond to these human experiences. Some time after the event he recounts, Vertosick notes that:

> when adverted after the event, these drugs can ... render a patient amnesic, with no recollection of the painful event at all. ... The thought of having open-heart surgery while fully awake and totally paralyzed must rank as one of the most awful images the average intellect can conjure. Nevertheless, with the appropriate amnesic agent, we wouldn't remember any of it, so why should it matter?
>
> (2000: 215)

The question concerning the ways that pain and suffering *matter*—not only for healthcare workers but for the rest of us as we attempt to understand and respond to these experiences in our own lives and those with whom we share our lives—is not ancillary to the phenomena of pain, but part and parcel of them. The self-evident (if negative) *value* of pain is the focus of this book.

Chronic Pain

One of the most fundamental social changes in the past century is population aging, particularly in the developed world, and with this phenomenon people spend more of their lives dealing with chronic illness and chronic pain. In fact, much of this book will focus on chronic rather than acute pain because chronic pain is the site of the problem of pain in our time. The scenes Hemingway and Vertosick recount represent acute pain: pain, technically speaking, that endures for less than six months (e.g., a broken leg, a surgical operation). Recent studies seem to indicate that *chronic pain*—defined as pain that extends beyond normal recovery time, is cyclical, like a migraine headache, or lasts longer than six months—produces a significantly different physiological response from that of acute pain (see Hardcastle 1999: 84), and in any case it is far more difficult to treat. Moreover, chronic pain has been described as an "epidemic" (Morris 1991: 20) and "a specter in our time" (Thernstrom 2010: 5; see Exhibit 1.1). As we will see, since the late nineteenth century science has developed very effective strategies to deal with acute pain: Vertosick's narrative makes this clear. However, adequate pain remedies for chronic pain, even today, are usually not available or not effective.

The reasons for this are both a function of physiology, but also a function of the particular *experience* of chronic pain. Chronic pain more fully provokes suffering rather than simple, acute pain, particularly if we define suffering, as I will in this book, as the felt and even accomplished threat of the destruction of a person's sense of her life as a whole. In a powerful autobiographical account of chronic illness, Lous Heshusius describes how, as her chronic pain became "hellish, a different person

---

EXHIBIT 1.1

In *The Pain Chronicles* Melanie Thernstrom adds that one study "in the United States indicates that as much as 44 percent of the population experiences pain on a regular basis, and nearly one in five people describes himself or herself as having had pain for three months or more. Much of the degraded quality of life from diseases such as cancer, diabetes, multiple sclerosis, and arthritis stems from persistent pain. In one survey, most chronic pain patients said that their pain was 'a normal part of their medical condition and something with which they must live.' One-third of the patients said that their pain's severity was 'sometimes so bad [they] want to die.' Almost one-half said they would spend all they have on treatment if they could be assured it would banish their pain" (2010: 6). In *Illness and Culture in the Postmodern Age* David Morris also notes that "every day one in six Americans is in pain. The National Center for Health Statistics estimated that in 1988 . . . nineteen percent of Americans were partially disabled by pain for periods of weeks or months, while another 2 percent were permanently disabled" (1998: 110).

started to form itself inside the one I thought I was." As her pain got worse:

> this other person who began as an intruder gradually became the familiar one . . . The one who obliterates the past, torments the present, and makes the future unbearable before the fact. Bit by bit, it has become almost impossible for me to remember who I once was. . . . I had become someone else, a crumbled woman.
>
> (2009: 25–26)

Both pain and suffering are notable human experiences, but suffering, as Dr. Eric Cassell notes, is best understood as a response to a serious threat to one's "personhood," those aspects of someone's life that vitally define them as a human person (1991: 160). This is what Heshusius's narrative, *Inside Chronic Pain*, describes. Needless to say, acute pain can have this effect—such a threat is the motor and object of torture—but it can be argued that this threat to personhood is almost always at the heart of chronic pain. In Hemingway's story, the young pregnant woman's husband commits suicide in the face of his wife's pain, which his action suggests he understands as a state of affairs rather than a momentary event, and the physician's son—a young boy of about six or seven years old, one can surmise—is left, at the end of the story, with a series of questions for his father about pain and death and with the childish thought "in the early morning on the lake sitting in the stern of the boat with his father rowing, he felt quite sure he would never die" (1970: 21). As usual, Hemingway doesn't tell us quite what is going on, but it is easy to surmise that this event has come to haunt the man the boy grows to be (the description of the boat's "stern" seems beyond the childish vocabulary of the boy), not necessarily as an instance of suffering, but as something that might occasion suffering, as opposed to pain.

The Representation of Pain

Linked to the issue of pain—both acute and chronic—is the manner in which it is grasped, the *representation* of pain. Dr. Vertosick recounts an anecdote when pain is not "grasped," at least not retrospectively, and therefore is felt not to exist, and most people who study pain assert that *by definition pain is conscious*. Moreover, the study of meaning in the humanities and the human sciences equally suggests that meaning—and the representational schemas and strategies examined in this book that condition meaning—is part of human consciousness (see Damasio 1999; Wittgenstein 2001; Edelman 2005; Schleifer 2009). In a very influential book in the humanities studying pain, *The Body in Pain*, Elaine Scarry (1985) offers an extended analysis and meditation on the fact that pain— particularly the pain of torture—"unmakes the world" by destroying, among other things, the possibility of discourse and representation. Such destruction is clear in Heshusius's account of her almost decade-long experiences of severe chronic pain or the notes of Alphonse Daudet (a French novelist of the late nineteenth century) on his equally long-lived painful experiences with tertiary syphilis. Daudet, for instance, asks and answers a question concerning the discursive representation of pain: "Are words actually any use to describe what pain (or passion, for that matter) really feels like? Words only come when everything is over, when things have calmed down. They refer only to memory, and are either powerless or untruthful" (2002: 15). The editor of Daudet's book, *In the Land of Pain*, Julian Barnes, adds a footnote describing Daudet's friend, the great novelist Marcel Proust, recounting the *speechlessness* of his own pain in comparison to Daudet's: "I remember to what extent bodily pain, so slight compared to his that no doubt he would have enjoyed it as a respite, had made me deaf and blind to other people, to life, to everything except my wretched body" (2002: 15).

These authors' struggles to represent and account for the pain that they suffer seem to substantiate Scarry's argument that pain destroys meaning and representation. Still, in important ways, pain is not simply private, but "an invitation to a dialogue" (Jackson 2002: 117). That is, third-person accounts of pain and suffering do allow for possibilities of discourse and representation. (This is particularly important in relation to patient–physician interaction, where a focus on the patient's concern, as well as the physician's knowledge, is of the utmost importance. This is an important aspect of Chapter 7 of this book.) Thus, in Dr. Paul Brand's third-person depictions of the sufferings of lepers or of a young girl afflicted by a rare defect known as "congenital indifference to pain" (1997: 5) he describes the physical disfigurations suffered by people who do not feel pain in a catalogue of amputations, dislocations, extremities behaving as physical objects rather than body parts. Such descriptions provoke, in me at least, the *cringing* we often feel when we encounter people in pain or even about to have an accident, a response such as we experience when we see a child fall off a bicycle. Here is one of his descriptions, representing a man with leprosy:

> I could tell from the man's gait, though, that something was badly wrong. Walking toward him, I saw that the bandages were wet with blood and his left foot flopped freely from side to side. By running on an already dislocated ankle, he had put far too much force on the end of his leg bone, and the skin had broken under the stress. He was walking on the end of his tibia, and with every step that naked bone dug into the ground. Nurses scolded the man sharply, but he seemed quite proud of himself for having run so fast. I knelt beside him and found that small stones and twigs had jammed through the end of the bone into the marrow cavity. I had no choice but to amputate the leg below the knee.
>
> (1997: 7)

Brand's physical descriptions of *situations* of pain—like Daudet's description of an excruciating painful treatment for his condition, physicians hanging him from his jaw to loosen up his spine, the part of his body from which much of his pain originated (2002: 30)—produce a *visceral* reaction, a kind of harrowing experience we often have when we encounter someone in pain. In the 1990s, neurologists discovered a way of accounting for this experience under the category of "mirror neurons" that fire not only when a person (and primates as well) perform a certain action, such as eating or stubbing a toe, but also fire when they see another person or member of their species eat: "when we see someone else suffering or in pain, mirror neurons help us to read her or his facial expression and actually make us feel the suffering or pain of the other person" (Iacoboni 2009: 4). Furthermore, Marco Iacoboni—in whose laboratory mirror neurons were first discovered—cites another neurological study that demonstrated that "areas in the brain known to control the movements of particular body parts (i.e., the hand or the mouth) were activated not only when subjects watched the movement on video but also when subjects read sentences about the movement" (2009: 94). This scientific work seems to account, by means of neuro-physiological events, for *representational* experience and meaning, both for the phenomena of empathy and the phenomena of vicarious experience. The doctor in Hemingway's story does not respond to his patient's pain in such a visceral fashion—in many ways, he was trained not to—even if we can see (and *feel*) in Hemingway's vivid description that his young son does. Thus, the voicelessness of pain within its human subject, which Scarry and Daudet describe, does not quite capture the ways that physical representations of pain (and in the case of Brand, of simply the situation of pain) allow for a *complex* sense of pain as both a (factual) event and a (human) experience; it does not quite capture pain as a *social* phenomenon. It might well be, as Scarry and Daudet suggest, that pain experience is, in important ways, unrepresentable, but the event of pain itself lends itself to representation, which, in some cases, provokes harrowing response. The representations of events and situations of pain allows one to grasp the threat to "personhood" that Cassell describes—the threat to the very physical existence of an integral person—and thus to represent and provoke suffering, which cannot be fully separated from pain as such.

Science and the Humanities

This short discussion of pain and its representations leads me to what brought me to focus on pain. A good number of the studies of pain I have encountered, as I have already suggested, in one way another *begin* with the authors' experiences of pain: either in their own lives, especially under the condition of chronic pain, or, as healthcare workers, in the lives of their patients and their profession. Although like virtually everyone, I have experienced pain in my life, I come to pain from neither perspective. (For this reason, throughout this book I generously cite people who have these more intimate engagements with pain in their lives.) Rather, I came to study pain from my work in the medical humanities. For more than a decade I have been teaching, together with my friend and colleague, Dr. Jerry Vannatta, a course in "Literature and Medicine" whose aim, in significant part, is to train people committed to work in the healthcare professions to gain new strategies for listening and responding to those in distress. Early in my work in this area, I became fascinated by Tourette Syndrome (TS) precisely because it is a clearly physiological dysfunction that manifests itself in cultural symptoms: people with certain forms of TS involuntarily blurt out words and phrases that are culturally prohibited in particular situations, *culturally transgressive* language. In our culture it often manifests itself in coprolalia, the eruption of cursing and/or obscene discourse. But in some cultures, it takes different forms of transgression, such as addressing people with familiar rather than formal pronouns. Even in our culture, the physiological dysfunction of TS can find different modes of transgression. In a detailed history of TS, Dr. Howard Kushner offers a narrative of a person with Tourette's blurting out, as he makes an airplane reservation, "There's a bomb on the plane!" (1999: 2). "It seems bizarre on the face of it," Kushner writes:

> that something as rooted in culture as the utterance of inappropriate phrases or obscene words could be attached to organic disease. What in some societies are viewed as outrageous curses are seen as inoffensive in others. Moreover, even within the same societies words lose their offensive connotations over time. What is most interesting about coprolalia in Tourette's sufferers is that they invoke the most inappropriate curse of their particular times and cultures.
>
> (1999: 7)

This curious combination of an organic-physiological dysfunction—the symptoms of TS are consistently reduced by dopamine-blocking drugs (see Stevens and Blachly 1966; Kushner 1999: 133–43)—and culturally determined behavior is a precise place where the objects of the sciences and the humanities are "integrated." (As I suggest below, I take "cultural studies" to be a central aspect of the humanities.) My interest in Tourette Syndrome led me to focus on the complex relationships among physiology, evolution, and cultural meanings in my recent work (2009; Schleifer and Vannatta 2013).

The phenomenon of pain is another such "place" where manifestations of physiology, evolutionary biology, and symbolic apprehension inextricably work together in its experience and understanding. Even more than TS—perhaps because pain is a ubiquitous rather than a rare phenomenon—pain *cannot* be understood outside a framework of understanding that integrates the sciences and the humanities. The sciences of pain—anatomy, neurology, psychology, even epidemiology— have developed a remarkably fine-textured understanding of the mechanics and biological functioning of pain in humans and other mammals. And in the development of anesthetics, pharmaceutics, and other attempts at "pain management," more or less precise scientific procedures and understanding have brought remarkable relief to countless numbers of people. The humanities of pain—its representations in the arts, its history, its philosophical analyses, and gathering these together, analyses of the *experience* of pain in cultural studies—has been less pragmatically focused, yet the relief it affords us, though perhaps less easily measured than those of the sciences, are also palpable and real. In fact, throughout history philosophers have focused on human pain in relation to what one philosopher calls "the hard problems of consciousness" (Grahek 2001: 155), precisely because pain is a *defining instance* of the nature of consciousness and experience altogether.

Moreover, across all known cultures, the representation of pain and its understanding within the context of human life—and, indeed, as a central part of the definitions of life itself—can be found everywhere. In the western tradition, when Aristotle imagined the importance of the systematic study of literature in *The Poetics*—one of the first disciplined attempts to account for the experience of art in the west, which is to say one of the first instances of the disciplined study of the humanities and cultural studies—he virtually begins by taking up a medical vocabulary concerned with confronting pain to describe the representation of pain and suffering in tragedy, specifically the "catharsis" or "purging" of pity and terror. In *The Portrait of the Artist as a Young Man*, James Joyce's central character, Stephen Dedalus, tries to more precisely define Aristotle's terms:

> Pity is the feeling that arrests the mind in the presence of whatsoever is grave and constant in human sufferings and unites it with the human sufferer. Terror is the feeling which arrests the mind in the presence of whatsoever is grave and constant in human sufferings and unites it with the secret cause.
>
> (1966: 204)

Science pursues the "secret cause" of suffering and pain; in the natural sciences, it attempts to apprehend causes behind phenomena and, in the social sciences, the patterns and trends in which phenomena manifest themselves. The humanities and cultural studies focus on the human sufferer; they attempt to arouse and comprehend both pity and terror in the face of experiences of pain and suffering.

In no place are these attentions and pursuits more fully integrated than in the confrontation and study of physical pain and human suffering. This is so not only because of the combination of empathetic and causal understanding, but because human pain itself—much more starkly than a disease like TS—is a site of human *experience*. This is clear in Dr. Vertosick's narrative, but historians, philosophers, people working in cultural studies—even psychologists and sociologists working in the social sciences—repeatedly focus on events of pain as experience: thus, one historian argues that the "anatomical and physiological foundation" of pain makes it "not an historical subject in the same sense as fear, or hell, or purgatory," but rather the site of the "one experience where the human condition's universality and the species' biological unity is manifest" (Rey 1993: 5); and philosophers from Aristotle to Wittgenstein make pain the object of their analyses (Hardcastle 1999: 95). In addition, one study of the phenomena of pain in religious experiences explicitly describes what the vast majority of thinkers focused on pain assume, that pain "is conscious by definition" (Glucklich 2001: 96); and another cultural study of pain asserts even more strongly that "one of the most obvious qualities of pain" is the fact that "it requires a consciousness to feel it. What the unconscious patient feels as the knife cuts into him is unknown, but it's not what we call pain" (Jackson 2002: 18). Still, as noted in Part I, the very definition of pain is a subject of controversy. That is, there are a number of philosophers who, taking the lead from what they assume is a strict "scientific" approach to the analysis of pain, disagree with the notion that experience is a *defining* feature of pain. Thus, Valerie Gray Hardcastle points out in a detailed neurological analysis of pain "the mistake [of] identifying pain with the experience of pain" [1999: 162]; and Nikola Grahek, in his book *Feeling Pain and Being in Pain* similarly argues for the distinction of his title, namely that the experience ["feeling"] of pain is not all there is to the fact/event of pain. (For a detailed and somewhat technical discussion of the relationship between the assumptions and methods of the sciences and humanities/cultural studies in analyses of pain, see Appendix I, "Pain, Science, and the Humanities." Appendix I pursues a somewhat formal discussion of the manner in which the study of human pain instantiates and requires the integration of science and culture.)

When researchers assert that "pain requires a consciousness to feel it," they call into question the simple notion of *passive* experience (including the passive experience of the stimulus-response model of pain). Instead, they suggest that at the heart of human experience is *active engagement* insofar as experience so conceived is not simply the passive or automatic response to stimuli, but an active engagement that, in relation to so-called stimuli, works to condition the nature of those stimuli itself. Such active engagement is particularly true in relation to pain. Thus, Patrick Wall notes that "the brain does not sit passively reading the sensory [pain] messages sent to it from the tissues and spinal cord. It sends out descending control systems which shape the received messages" (1999: 56). More colorfully, Dr. Scott Fishman notes that pain (and I should add the schemas and neurological subroutines that give rise to and shape the experience of pain described later in this book) "does more than ring a bell—it hammers the bell into a new shape" (2000: 85). (Wall, a neuroscientist, and Fishman, a pain specialist, are, as we shall see, major researchers in the phenomenon of human pain; we will encounter them throughout this book.) Most importantly, the active engagement of experience entails action in the world. Thus, Wall suggests that the brain's response to sensory pain input focuses on "what action would be appropriate" under the circumstances of pain (1999: 176); and more generally, information processing in the brain in sensory systems is almost always related to the motor system insofar as our brains evolved to be adaptive for living and acting in the world (see Hardcastle 1999: 99, 100). Thus, most, if not all, of what the humanities study is related directly or indirectly to action in the world.

The combination of knowledge and action is starkly clear, as I hope this book demonstrates, in relation to the phenomenon of pain and its complex existence as both a fact/event and an experience, a sensation and a perception. Moreover, its complexity is governed both by inherited schemas in relation to neurological subroutines and acquired schemas based upon our ability (shared with the cultures into which we are born) to apprehend patterns of facts/events. That is, pain is always a *physiological event*—even when it does not present a physiological cause (i.e., in the case of "psychogenic" pain)—and also a *meaningful experience* that occasions and provokes action in the world. In fact, one working definition of suffering is the inability to grasp possibilities of acting in the world: this is part of what Scarry means by "unmaking the world." Moreover, because pain is an all-but-unavoidable event and experience for us all, it most clearly delineates the integration of science and culture. That is, as Vertosick's amnesic agents vividly suggest, the experience and the fact/event of pain are intimately connected. This connection requires the integration of science and culture in the study of and in active responses to pain and suffering.

The Structure of This Book

This book is organized into three parts. Part I, "The Nature of Pain," examines physiological and phenomenological features of human pain. (*Phenomenology* is the study of how objects and events are experienced and encountered rather than the nature of objects and events in themselves.) Chapter 2 focuses on the by and large uncontroversial physiology of nerve transmission of pain "signals" by means of pain-sensitive nociceptive nerves, the spine, and brain areas that both react to and re-signal pain messages; and Chapter 3 examines the phenomena of chronic pain, which have led to a greater sense of controversy about what takes place in the fact/event/experience of pain. Finally, Chapter 4 surveys treatments of pain—anesthetics, analgesics, and non-invasive pain treatments such as the placebo effect, hypnosis, palliative care— with the aim of shedding light on the nature of pain by examining strategies to relieve pain.

Part II, "Experiences of Pain," focuses more directly on pain conceived of as experience rather than sensation. Chapter 5 examines various senses of the *quality* of pain experience, including systematic measurements of pain thresholds and pain tolerance; the ways in which schemas condition the felt experiences of pain; the ways in which pain experience occurs in relation to cultural formations. Such cultural formations are organized around particular schemas, which create for groups of people living in the same time and space the very *horizon* of experience, more or less unconscious (or unreflected upon) assumptions about the world that create specific forms of attention and expectation that contribute to and condition experiences of pain. Chapter 5 also offers a strong working definition of *suffering* that both distinguishes it from the felt-experience of pain and demonstrates the link between pain and suffering; and it ends by examining particular "intensifiers" of pain that suggest ways in which healthcare workers and others living with pain might themselves bring certain forms of attention and expectation to their engagements with terrible experiences of pain. If Chapter 5 focuses, more or less, on private or individual experiences of pain (even when they are conditioned by social and cultural schemas of attention and expectation), Chapter 6 focuses more fully on social experiences of pain. To this end, it examines biases in relation to the experiences of pain, particularly in widely held social attitudes towards the pain of infants and of women; it examines the "political" uses of pain in practices of torture; it focuses on representations of pain, particularly within rituals and belief systems of religion; and it ends by returning to the seemingly self-evident opposition of pleasure and pain.

Part III, "Living with Pain," focuses on the implications that the definition and analyses of *Pain and Suffering* have for healthcare workers and other caretakers (including sufferers themselves) engaged with people suffering from pain. Its single chapter, "Caretakers and Sufferers Dealing with Pain," revisits the definitions of pain and suffering that have been examined throughout this book with an eye towards creating strategies for action in the world that I argue earlier in this chapter are part of the work of integrating science and culture in the study of pain. The short Appendix I also pursues a discussion of the integration of science and culture to the ends of understanding and effective action. Appendix II presents a catalogue of online resources focused on pain. (Some of these resources are directly related to the ways that sufferers of chronic pain can "construct a sense of themselves and of themselves in relation to others" [Barker 2002:83] as active responses to their pain that sociologists have recorded). Bringing together science and culture, as I have already suggested, might accomplish at least to some extent my great hope for this book: to help shape horizons of understanding, empathy, and action to the end of mitigating the pain and suffering that are part and parcel of the lives we live.

PART I
THE NATURE OF PAIN

2

THE PHYSIOLOGY OF PAIN: HOW THE BODY WORKS

We naively believed that pain is simple—it hurts or it doesn't hurt—so there should be a single brain state we could see every time someone is in pain. But what we've stumbled into is the discovery that there's a relative universe of hurt—that hurting is an immense, rich, and varied human experience, associated with an unknown number of possible brain states. From a scientific position, we're overwhelmed at how large that universe is. We're still at the stage where each step forward makes us realize how far we have to go.

—Dr. John Keltner, pain therapist
(cited in Thernstrom 2010: 324)

Despite the fact that human beings have lived with pain from time immemorial, there remains a great deal of controversy concerning its nature and its meaning. Before the modern era, pain was understood across many cultures as a sign for something else: punishment, a message from the gods, a measure of payment, etc. In our own time, pain has been variously understood as simply a symptom for some other concomitant condition, a disease in its own right, a neurological sub-system comparable to other sensory systems such as sight or hearing,

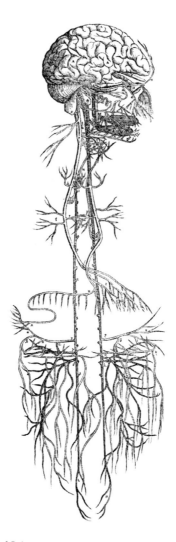

Figure 2.1 The Physiology of Pain

a psychological rather than a physical state, a physical rather than a psychological state, etc. Thus while there is great consensus concerning the cellular and, to a lesser extent, neurological physiology of pain in our time, there is also great controversy over the details of the physiology of pain and its place in the larger economy of human life. This chapter presents agreed-upon descriptions of the nature of the fact/event of pain; the following chapter examines areas of controversy concerning the physiology and meaning of pain in human life.

Definitions of Pain

In the last half century or so we have come to understand a great deal about pain as a physiological fact/event. Still, that physiological fact, as we shall see throughout this book, is strongly connected to the experiential phenomena of memory and anticipation—*attention and expectation* that are conditioned by schemas of experience—and more generally, as Dr. John Keltner says, with brain states associated with those experiential phenomena. In this, as noted in Chapter 1, the scientific study of pain has understood it as both a physiological fact/event and a phenomenological experience. (As already mentioned, phenomenology is the study of how the world is experienced rather than its nature outside of experience.) There is a neuro-physiological basis for this distinction of pain as a fact/event and as an experience, a distinction that is of the utmost importance in this book. That is, there is evidence for different neurological mechanisms for "procedural memory," the memory of motor functions such as riding a bicycle, and "episodic memory," the memory of specific events of experience such as a particular Sunday on which one rode in a bike race (see Donald 1991: 150–51, Ornstein 1997; Schleifer 2009: 142–45). This distinction suggests that pain exists as both an episodic memory—it is something that "happens" to a person—*and* it can also produce the seemingly simple fact of procedural or implicit memory, such as the automatic favoring of a limb or the tightening of back muscles even beyond the healing time of an injured disk. In this way pain is both an experienced event and a seeming automatic state of affairs. As suggested in Chapter 1 in the example of Hemingway's story, physicians are often trained to overlook the experience/perception of pain in favor of the condition associated with it. Such training in large part takes acute pain as the model for all pain, and in so doing mistakes the nature of chronic pain and, sometimes, mistakes the nature of suffering. Not only does Hemingway's doctor ignore his patient's screams, he ignores any possible suffering it might give rise to in her family.

The International Association for the Study of Pain defines pain as "an unpleasant sensory and emotional experience associated with actual or potential tissue damage or described in terms of such damage"; and the IASP goes on to define it in some detail:

> The inability to communicate verbally does not negate the possibility that an individual is experiencing pain and is in need of appropriate pain-relieving treatment. Pain is always subjective. Each individual learns the application of the word through experiences related to injury in early life. Biologists recognize that those stimuli which cause pain are liable to damage tissue. Accordingly, pain is that experience we associate with actual or potential tissue damage. It is unquestionably a sensation in a part or parts of the body, but it is also always unpleasant and therefore also an emotional experience. Experiences which resemble pain but are not unpleasant, e.g., pricking, should not be called pain. Unpleasant abnormal experiences (dysesthesias [an impairment of the senses, particularly touch]) may also be pain but are not necessarily so because, subjectively, they may not have the usual sensory qualities of pain. Many people report pain in the absence of tissue damage or any likely pathophysiological cause; usually this happens for psychological reasons. There is usually no way to distinguish their experience from that due to tissue damage if we take the subjective report. If they regard their experience as pain, and if they report it in the same ways as pain caused by tissue damage, it should be accepted as pain. This definition avoids tying pain to the stimulus. Activity induced in the nociceptor [pain receptor nerves] and nociceptive pathways by a noxious stimulus is not pain, which is always a psychological state, even though we may well appreciate that pain most often has a proximate physical cause.
>
> (IASP website)

As we shall see, there is some controversy whether this psychological/subjective definition of pain is correct. Thus, the philosopher Valerie Gray Hardcastle argues that the brain states that give rise to the experience of pain can better be described in neuro-physiological rather than psychological terms.

Patrick Wall, who (often along with Ronald Melzack) helped shape the study of pain in the mid-twentieth century, nicely describes the *physiological fact* of pain in a larger context. "Pain," he proposes, "occurs as the brain is analysing the situation [that gave rise to pain] in terms of actions that might be appropriate" (1999: 169; see also 177); "pain," he says, "is then best seen as a need state, like hunger and thirst, which are terminated by a consummatory act" (1999: 183). As a need state, pain is an experience that—like the experiences studied by the humanities—*gives rise to action*. The appropriate action pain provokes, however, unlike hunger and thirst, is not directed toward objects in the world (food or drink), but rather focuses on states of the body— the *location of pain*—and on brain states that give rise to the experience of pain.

In another definition, Dr. Scott Fishman, Chief of the Division of Pain Medicine, UC Davis, past President of the American Pain Foundation and past President of the American Academy of Pain Medicine, elaborates on Wall's description. In an "incomplete understanding," he writes (using the "alarm" metaphor he often repeats):

> most of us think of pain as a sensation or a perception of a noxious stimulus. Pain is the alarm system in the human body that tells us about imminent harm, actual harm, or healing. The alarm system is connected to measurable biological and physio- logical responses that are associated with distinct molecules and cells in the body. However, that is not all that is involved in pain. Pain is a multidimensional phenomenon that integrates perception with emotion to form the complex experience of suffering. Although you can identify the precipitating event, the end result is like a symphony in which you are able to hear the themes but unable to distinguish all of the many instruments.
> (2009: 132; see also 2000: esp. 5–51)

Pain, in this account, has three adaptive functions: to warn us of imminent harm (so that by "automatic reflex," we remove our toes from a burning coal *to avoid* tissue damage [see Hardcastle 1999: 67–69 for a neuro-physiological description of reflex behavior]), to respond quickly to actual harm (so that we remove our burnt finger from a fire *to prevent* additional, irreparable tissue damage), and to promote healing (so that we "favor" injured parts of the body *to evade* exacerbation of the damage).

Others describe two rather than three functions: (1) the avoidance system and (2) the restorative or repair system (Grahek: 2001: 9). Studying asymbolia, a rare neurological condition where "patients feel pain upon harmful stimulation, but their pain no longer represents danger or threat to them" (2001: xii), Nikola Grahek suggests that the complex phenomenon of pain, which includes the *perception* of threat as well as physical *sensation*, cannot be understood as just simple (or "pure") sensation. That is, he argues that asymbolia offers an example of:

> the very essence of pain; that the pure juice of pain quality—
> the what-it-is-likeness of pain—has been extracted [from its
> affective and motivational aspects] and clearly presented. But
> . . . the pure juice or essence of pain experience thus extracted
> has turned out to be a blunt, fleshless, inert sensation pointing
> to nothing beyond itself, leaving no traces in the memory and
> powerless to move the body and mind in any way. Moreover,
> when reduced to pure sensation, pain becomes the object of
> ridicule.
>
> (2001: 78)

As we see in these various (and somewhat controversial) definitions, there is much attention to the distinction between what Fishman calls the "sensation" and "perception" of pain: the combination in the event and experience of pain of more or less "objective" stimulation and more or less "subjective" perception. (Such stimulation, as suggested in Chapter 1, is often assumed to be passively received.) But despite this essential controversy related to pain, science—anatomy and more recently neurology—has nicely traced the physiology of these pain functions, and this chapter describes this tested and consensual knowledge.

As already mentioned in Chapter 1, the noxious phenomenon of pain—whatever its combination of sensation and perception—"is conscious by definition" (Glucklich 2001: 96). In fact, it has been noted by a pioneer in pain studies that *"nothing can properly be called pain unless it can be consciously perceived as such"* (Livingston 1998: 141). Moreover, pain is literally and materially marked and inscribed in damaged tissue. That is, the memory of pain—like memory in general—has been shown to be a *biological* process in cellular mechanisms through which pain is physiologically and psychologically remembered. (We should also recall the strange phenomenon of "amnesiac" anesthesia mentioned in Chapter 1 where such memory is erased.) That is, pain itself stimulates cellular mechanisms that allow even brief noxious stimuli to persistently alter the material state of actual cells and thus the nervous system itself, which may lead to central sensitization within the dorsal horn of the spine, the brain stem, the brain, and perhaps even peripheral sensitization in pain-receptor nerves or "nociceptors" (physiological sites of pain stimuli described later in this chapter). In even primitive organisms external impressions are laid down within the body itself, leading to predispositions and tendencies to feel and react in a certain way (Hilts 1995: 28). The phrase "laid down" means that stimuli-experiences (here the combination of sensation and perception) are actually, materially *marked* in the body. In 2000 Eric Kandel won the Nobel Prize in Physiology or Medicine for his work on the mechanics of memory storage in neurons by focusing on a single sensory neuron and a single motor neuron of the giant invertebrate sea snail, aplysia. His research group found that "a shock to the tail activates modulatory interneurons that release serotonin, thereby strengthening the [synaptic] connections between sensory neurons and motor neurons" by creating the growth of new synaptic connections, "an anatomical change [involving] the synthesis of new protein" (2006: 254, 256). In other words, the ways in which noxious stimuli led to the physiological alteration of a neuron was demonstrated: neurons are materially transformed by new growth. The phenomena Kandel describes participate in a long-time understanding of pain—going back to René Descartes at the beginning of the Enlightenment in the seventeenth century—in relation to a model of stimulus and response: in pain, a noxious stimulus creates a physiological and affective ("feeling") response, understood as an instance of the simple (i.e., *passively* one directional) stimulus-response model proposed by Descartes and later by mechanistic behaviorism in the early twentieth century. It is this understanding of pain that governs the physician's response in Hemingway's story, where pain doesn't seem important once it fulfills its "alarm" function. Within this stimulus-response model—one, alas, shared by too many physicians—pain is simple: it is the "alarm" symptom of one sort or another that Fishman describes, automatic and passive, and, outside its existence as a symptom *of something else*, it is simply meaningless.

The connection between sensory neurons and motor neurons Kandel studies is of the utmost importance to the *adaptive* function of pain: that is, the sensation or perception of pain is necessarily closely connected to *action in the world*, and as mentioned in Chapter 1, the work of the humanities, insofar as they focus on experience, often develops strategies of *action* in the world as well as studying, as the physical and social sciences do, simple states of affairs. (Needless to say, the physical and social sciences often strongly imply strategies of action. See Appendix I for a more detailed examination of these sciences in relation to the humanities and cultural studies.) Moreover, this explicit focus in the humanities/cultural studies on the relation between experience and action helps us grasp how the physiological "memory" of pain—"procedural" or "implicit" memory—can create all sorts of problems discussed later in this book: it creates anticipated pain that disorganizes stable muscular activities, "favoring" a sore ankle as we say, in our physical interactions with the world; it threatens and sometimes disrupts our sense of personhood and integrity; it disrupts language in our verbal interactions with the world; and there is good evidence it can give rise to neuropathological conditions where pain does not function adaptively as an alarm for imminent damage, actual damage, and the healing of damage, but instead becomes a *disease* in its own right, neurological dysfunction that occasions chronic pain without any protective functioning.

The Physiology of Pain

The physiological events of pain are relatively well understood, especially on the level of nerve cells. Pain is conditioned in relation to the interaction of the three major components of the nervous system: the peripheral nerves, the spinal cord, and the brain. The peripheral nerves include pain receptors or "nociceptors," which are receptors that detect actual or potential tissue damage. They exist not only in interface with the environment associated with skin, cornea, mucosa membranes, but also internally, associated with muscles, joints, bladder, gut. Nociceptors, located in the skin and other tissues, are nerve fibers that can be excited by three types of stimuli: mechanical, thermal, and chemical; some respond primarily to one type of stimulation, while other nerve endings can detect all types. Patrick Wall notes that:

> the skin is profusely innervated with three types of sensory fibres. One group, called A beta fibres, are wrapped in a fatty protein called myelin and are sensitive to gentle pressure. The second group, called A delta fibres, are thinner and are sensitive to heavy pressure and temperature. The third group, called C fibres, are very thin and have no myelin, and respond to pressure, chemicals and temperature. Deep tissue organs such as the heart, bladder and gut are innervated only by the thinner fibres.
> . . . Some of our sensory nerve fibres are more than a metre long, running from the toes to the middle of the back; others are only a few centimetres long, running from the teeth to the hind brain.
>
> (1999: 40)

For detailed physiological descriptions of A fibers and C fibers, see Grahek 2001: ch. 8; for the experiences that stimulating these fibers give rise to, see Thernstrom 2010: 27; see Exhibit 2.1.

The A-delta fiber "sensory discriminative" subsystem "computes the location, intensity, duration, and nature (stabbing, burning, prickling) of the stimuli" while the "'affective motivational' subsystem" begins with the C fibers. The two systems of response—with the C-fiber system phylogenetically older—are "similar to the color and form processors in the visual system . . . [and] remain largely segregated" (Hardcastle 1999: 102–03; *phylogeny* is the study of evolutionary divergence of species in relation to their common ancestors). Although these physiological facts are widely accepted, the language of "sensory discriminative" vs. "affective motivational" subsystems that Hardcastle uses here is part of her more

EXHIBIT 2.1

Properties of Different Afferent Fibers

	Myelinated		Unmyelinated
Fiber type	A-beta	A-delta	C
Conduction velocity	30–100 m/sec	6–30 m/sec	1.0–2.5 m/sec
Respond to*	light pressure	1 light pressure	1 light pressure
		2 heavy pressure	2 heavy pressure
		3 heat (45° C +)	3 heat (45° C +)
		4 chemicals	4 chemicals
		5 cooling	5 warmth

*Each fiber in the A-delta and C group may respond to only one or to more than one of the types of stimuli.

(adapted from Melzack and Wall 1983: 104)

controversial contention that a physiological rather than a psychological description of pain is more accurate. Nevertheless, there is general acceptance that these two aspects of pain—its sensory location and its motivational feelings—can be dissociated so that only one or the other operates, either by means of natural accidents or drugs, leading people to be able to localize pain sensations without becoming upset by the fact that they are in pain (as in the asymbolia Grahek describes) or, on the contrary, leading them to be able "to have a pain sensation . . . [while lacking] fine localization and intensity discrimination" (Hardcastle 1999: 104). Finally, the nociceptive centers in the thalamus and cortex can be activated without corresponding activations of A-delta or C fibers in phenomena such as much lower back pain (fully 80 percent of reported back pain is not associated with measurable tissue damage [Hardcastle 1999: 104]) or "phantom limb" pain in missing limbs described in Chapter 3.

The peripheral nerve fibers transmit pain messages to an area of the spinal cord called the dorsal horn in the forms of both electrically induced impulses (A-delta nociceptors) and chemical transmission (C-fiber nociceptors). Chemical transmission is much slower than electrical impulses, often taking hours or even days (Wall 1999: 41). In the spinal dorsal horn (located along much of the length of the spine), chemical neurotransmitters are released that activate other nerve cells in the spinal cord, which almost instantaneously transmit the pain messages up to the brain (at times via the reticular formation in the brain stem). More specifically, pain signals are transmitted to the thalamus, a subcortical area of the brain ("two walnut-sized bundles of nerves deep within the brain" [Fishman 2000: 88]). The thalamus quickly forwards the message simultaneously to three specialized regions of the brain: the somatosensory cortex (the physical sensation region), the limbic system (the emotional feeling region), and the frontal cortex (the region of cognitive activity). Wall notes that "no one area [of the brain] has the monopoly of capturing the one and only input signal associated with pain. One thing is certain: we are not going to find a single pain centre as proposed by Descartes" (1999: 56; see also Thernstrom 2010: 287 for a more detailed narrative of the neuronal and neural pathways of pain). This system of pain transmission has been called the *spinothalamic tract* (Hardcastle 1999: 175), which is mentioned in Chapter 4 in a discussion of surgical pain treatment. (See Exhibit 2.2.)

Following the parallels she traces among visual, auditory, and pain "sensory systems"—I use quotes here because many researchers do not categorize pain as a sensory system parallel to sight, hearing, taste— Hardcastle concludes that just as:

> the components of our visual system take the information contained in photons bouncing around in the world and use it to compute the location, orientation, texture, color, and movement of objects in the environment ... [and] components of our auditory system take the information contained in atmospheric compression waves and use it to compute the placement of things, [so] the components of our pain system take pressure, temperature, and chemical readings of our surface (and interior) and use this information to track what is happening to our tissues. The A-delta cells and the C-fibers do this, as do the spinothalamic tract and its connections to the cortex. In sum,

it appears we have a complex but well-defined sensory system
that monitors our tissues to promote the welfare of our bodies.

(1999: 107)

Although not all pain researchers pursue the analogy between pain and
other sensory systems that Hardcastle articulates here, I find this analogy
in her description of the functioning of the physiological pain system
informative and persuasive.

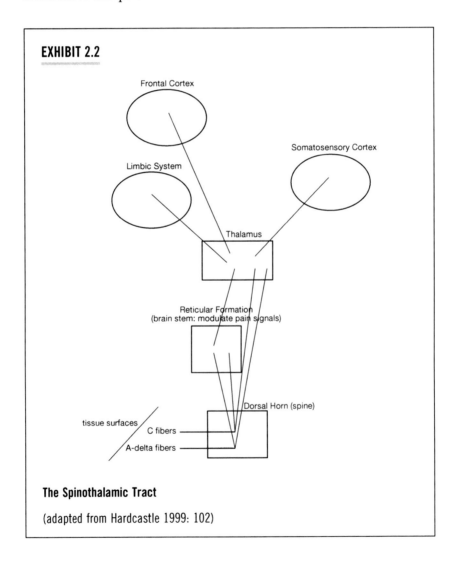

EXHIBIT 2.2

Frontal Cortex

Somatosensory Cortex

Limbic System

Thalamus

Reticular Formation
(brain stem: modulate pain signals)

Dorsal Horn (spine)

tissue surfaces

C fibers

A-delta fibers

The Spinothalamic Tract

(adapted from Hardcastle 1999: 102)

Since World War II—and in significant part due to the work of Wall and his colleague, Ronald Melzack—we have learned that the transmission of pain signals is not linear or straightforward. That is, pain messages do not travel directly from the pain receptors to the brain. Rather, when pain messages reach the spinal cord, they encounter specialized nerve cells that act as gatekeepers, which, governed by the brain, filter the pain messages on their way to the brain and even, in the case of weak pain messages, block them entirely. This has been called the Gate Control Theory of pain. Wall and Melzack developed Gate Control Theory in the 1960s. The theory, which has been "subsequently supported by numerous clinical studies, posits a mechanism in the spinal cord that controls the flow of neuronal stimuli from the body's peripheries to the brain, where pain registers." The gate-control mechanism, Melzack and Wall argued, operates by means of "inhibiting signals that 'descend' from the brain to the gate and block the incoming signals" (Glucklich 2001: 52–53; see also Melzack and Wall 1983: 222–39; Melzack 1993; Melzack 1995).

While acknowledging that some parts of the theory have been shown to be correct, Hardcastle argues against Gate Control Theory because, as noted in Chapter 3, she is convinced that a model of two separate neuro-physiological systems, the Pain Sensory System and the Pain Inhibiting System, more fully accounts for the complex event/experience of pain without positing the absolute opposition of mind and body that she believes the Gate Control Theory suggests. (Hardcastle's judgment is probably influenced by Melzack's later "neuromatrix theory" also discussed in Chapter 3. Even Wall, with whom Melzack developed the Gate Control Theory, was skeptical of Melzack's later theory.) More specifically, she takes the Gate Control Theory to describe a "top-down" cortical process insofar as the theory describes inhibition "descending" from the brain. In fact, such a top-down process is what she understands the IASP phrase "purely subjective" to mean (1999: 129). Throughout her analysis of pain, she argues for what I might call a "bottom-up process" that grounds its understanding of pain in terms of physiological rather than mental phenomena.

Still, good evidence suggests some kind of gate-keeping in relation to pain located in the spine. In relation to the case of "phantom" pain from missing limbs—a pain phenomenon focused upon in the next chapter—it seems that the specialized nerves of Gate Control Theory account for the transmission of pain messages even when there is no external source of pain (Vertosick 2000: 4–48; see also Wall 1999: 107). But whether or not the Melzack/Wall or the Hardcastle explanation more fully accounts for the physiology of pain, it is clear that pain messages can change within the peripheral nerves, the spinal cord, and the brain. Nerve cells in the spinal cord may release chemicals that intensify the pain, affecting the strength of the pain signal that reaches the brain. This is called wind-up or sensitization. With these mechanisms—whether they be a Gate Control or a Pain Inhibiting System (that includes pain enhancement)—rather than just reacting to pain, the brain actually generates messages that influence the perception of pain. The brain may signal nerve cells to release natural painkillers, such as endorphins or enkephalins, which diminish the pain messages. In this way, a simple stimulus-response model for pain does not account for what *happens*—physiologically and phenomenologically—in human pain.

A final physiological response to injury, which Wall calls the tertiary response (after the "immediate" and "secondary" responses of the A-delta and C fibers) is inflammation. Swelling, redness, heat, and pain are the classical signs of inflammation (Wall 1999: 43), and while inflammation hurts, it also heals in various ways: increasing blood flow, delivering nutrients to the injury site, and removing dead cells (Fishman 2000: 14; see also Thernstrom 2010: 27). Like the C fibers, inflammation is a response to damaged tissue that makes the area surrounding it sensitive, in part by releasing "a flood of chemicals including a peptide (a very small protein molecule) called bradykinin. Bradykinin swirls about, probably making your pain nerves more sensitive and creating tiny leaks in blood vessels in the neighborhood of the injury" (Fishman 2000: 41). Still, inflammation—like neuropathic pain sensitivity, which arises due to nerve damage or genetics (see Thernstrom 2010: 190)— sometimes becomes a disease itself, rather than a response to injury. It becomes a source of pain—often chronic pain, as in the case of inflammation-causing diseases such as rheumatoid arthritis—in its own right. It is notable that there are distinct physiological events in acute and chronic inflammation, just as there are differences in the transmission of pain signals that distinguish acute and chronic pain in general (Hardcastle 1999: 84). Moreover, the general physiological account of pain set forth in this chapter, particularly its three modalities associated with different fibers and inflammation, are most concerned with an episode of acute pain. As David Morris notes, "we cannot assume that chronic pain follows exactly the same model" (1991: 156; in addition to references already made, this discussion is based upon "How You Feel Pain"; and *The Encyclopedia Britannica* ["Physiology of Pain"; "Inflammation"]; see also Melzack and Wall 1983: Part Two; Morris 1991: 155–57; Melzack 1993; Damasio 1999: 71–74; and Wall 1999: ch. 3.) The next chapter pursues the examination of chronic pain, where the controversies latent in the definitions of pain described here become full-voiced.

3

THE PHENOMENON OF CHRONIC PAIN: CONTROVERSIES AND UNDERSTANDING

Pain is an *opinion* on the organism's state of health rather than a mere reflexive response to an injury. There is no direct hotline from pain receptors to "pain centers" in the brain. On the contrary, there is so much interaction between different brain centers, like those concerned with vision and touch, that even the mere visual appearance of an opening fist [in a mirror in the place of a missing hand] can actually feed all the way back into the patient's motor and touch pathways, allowing him to feel the [phantom] fist opening, thereby killing an illusory pain in a nonexistent hand.

—V.S. Ramachandran and Sandra Blakeslee,
Phantoms in the Brain (1998: 54)

Chronic Pain: Controversy beyond Consensus

The physiological bases of pain described in Chapter 2 focus most minutely on acute pain. But the *problem* of pain in our time—as a sensation and as a perception—has arisen in relation to the phenomena of *chronic pain*. In fact, most of the researchers on pain cited in this book focus on chronic pain because in the last century great strides have been made in alleviating acute pain and because the very knowledge of the

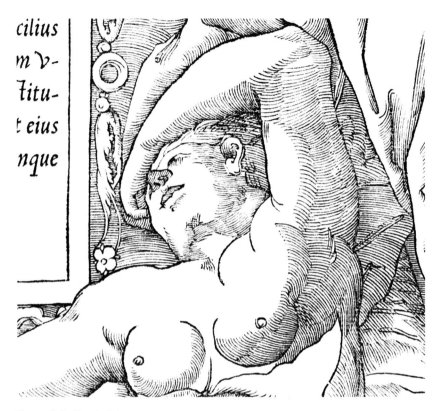

Figure 3.1 Chronic Pain

source and duration of acute pain makes its *experience* significantly different from chronic pain. Thus, it has been noted that "a majority of chronic pain sufferers have an affliction for which there is no known cause, little or medical help, and no good explanation for why they have the condition they do" (Hardcastle 1999: 10). In a more precise description, Dr. Scott Fishman articulates the *problem* of chronic pain when he observes that chronic pain does not alert a person to possible damage, but rather "is just ugly noise"; he further remarks that "acute pain is a symptom of disease; chronic pain itself is a disease" (2000: 53–54) and notes that such pain, as opposed to "the raw pain of a surgical patient . . . [is] woven into a person's personality" (2000: 112). Patrick Wall also notes that "chronic pain is more than prolonged acute pain"

(1999: 170); and David Morris powerfully asserts that "chronic pain and acute pain are as different as cancer and the common cold" (1991: 70). In these descriptions, as in many others focused on chronic pain, the simple, physiological functionality of pain as an alarm system breaks down. What arises in its stead is a heightened sense of the *suffering* associated with pain, which is more closely associated with pain as an experience/perception rather than as a simple sensation.

The preceding chapter described pain variously as a "sensation" or "perception." In this, it takes the lead from Fishman (but many others as well), who notes the paradoxical fact that pain is a sensation, but pain relief can occur "without changing the sensation that initially caused the pain" (2000: 98–99) so that the *perception* of pain is distinct from its *sensation*. (Among other occasions, this perception/experience of pain relief happens as a result of lobotomies, examined in Chapter 4, or the asymbolia that Nikola Grahek examines, which was mentioned earlier.) The alternative description of pain as a sensation *or* a perception subtly reinforces the opposition implicit in the IASP definition of pain as "always subjective" and as also "unquestionably a sensation in a part or parts of the body." More precise neurological study has begun to examine the neurological bases of sensation, perception, and emotion (while sometimes classifying emotion within the larger category of perception), although in these matters there is more controversy than consensus. In any case, the (somewhat controversial) description of pain as a perception rather than a simple sensation is closely linked to the phenomena of chronic pain insofar as chronic pain doesn't seem to *function* as a sensory system such as sight or hearing that simply seems to interact (however complex that interaction may be) with stimuli. Chronic pain seems to have a life of its own.

Controversy about the nature of pain goes back to ancient times. Aristotle, and classical western medicine more generally, assumed that pain was an emotion rather than a sensation. As such, it cannot simply be understood as a bodily response to the environment. In explicating Aristotle, Hardcastle argues that both emotions and perceptions come to us "unbidden." She asserts that it is difficult to distinguish among emotional, sensory, and cognitive responses in relation to pain: "they all run together in the brain" (1999: 114), and throughout her work she describes chronic pain "in terms of a perceptual-emotional mental unit" (1999: 118). In greater detail, Melanie Thernstrom argues that "anxiety and depression are not merely cognitive or affective responses to pain; they are physiologic consequences of it" (2010: 157), and like Hardcastle (and many others) she notes that pain is neither sensation nor emotion alone, but rather:

> the elusive intersection of three overlapping circles—cognition, sensation, and emotion. When any of these elements is missing, there is no pain. There is no such thing as being in pain without knowing you are. There is no such thing as being in pain without feeling the sensation of pain. And there is no such thing as pain that does not cause a salient emotional reaction.
>
> (2010: 284)

While this is true of pain in general, it is particularly true of chronic pain, which is the focus of Thernstrom's study.

Pain and the Brain: Sensation, Perception, and Modulation

Closely associated with the problem and complexity of chronic pain is the focused attention given to neurological processes associated with the phenomena of pain in more recent years insofar as such studies have tried to describe pain in relation to other sensory systems or, alternatively, in relation to larger cognitive systems. At one extreme is the philosophical analysis of pain based upon biological materialism—that is, based upon the neuro-physiology of the brain. Hardcastle nicely articulates this position in her attempt to debunk "two myths about pain": first, she denies that pain is a subjective state of mind; and second she denies that pain without any physiological corollary—which is sometimes called "psychopathological pains" or "psychogenic pain"—actually exists. (We can define psychogenic pain as "physical pain that is caused, augmented, or prolonged by emotional factors" [Thernstrom 2010: 140]). Both of these myths, Hardcastle argues, assume (often not fully explicitly) that there is "a pernicious dualistic mind/body distinction" in understanding the phenomenon of pain as a form of psychopathology that subscribes to the truth of the psychogenic claim that all pain is subjective. In opposition to this assumption Hardcastle argues "that all pains are physical and localizable and that all are created equal" (1999: 7).

Yet even within such a strict material-physiological description of pain Hardcastle does acknowledge evidence for another conception of the nature of pain, and in so doing she *enacts* the controversy between "objective" and "subjective" descriptions of pain. That is, in the midst of her strict *materialist* neurological description of pain, she concedes that:

> our emotional states heavily influence the degree of pain we feel, quite independent of actual injury. Indeed, "psychogenic" pains have been documented since the late 1800s, when D. H. Tuke reported the case of a butcher who got fouled up on a meat hook and appeared to be in agony. However, when examined by the local chemist [pharmacist], it was discovered that the meat hook had only penetrated his jacket sleeve and, even though the butcher was screaming in "excessive pain," he was completely unharmed.
>
> (1999: 104)

In a similar fashion, another strict materialist, Nikola Grahek, spends a good deal of time describing "painfulness without pain," by which he means (in part) subjects who have "lost the sensory-discriminative capacities of pain [and are] no longer able to precisely localize noxious stimuli" (2001: 110), what he later calls a "bizarre case of pain affect [emotion/perception] without pain sensation" (2001: 111). The key term here in both accounts is "localizable": with this term, Hardcastle and Grahek are arguing that there is *always* a material, physiological base for pain, even when it occurs as a "phantom" pain seemingly emanating from an absent limb.

To this end, Hardcastle describes the difference between chronic and acute pain in *physiological* terms, focused on the dorsal horn (1999: 84), and she also notes that chronic pain is "a perceptual-emotional mental unit" (1999: 118). More specifically, she describes chronic pain in terms of "schema theory," which was developed by psychology—and later in work in Artificial Intelligence—to provide systematic accounts of experience in terms of recurrent salient features of situations. A schema "is a high-level conceptual structure or framework that organizes prior experience and helps us to interpret new situations" (Gureckis and Goldstone 2011: 725); it is a framework that focuses *attention and expectation*. (See Exhibit 3.1.) Moreover, schema theory assumes the schemas of experience are *active structures* that "underlie both declarative [i.e., episodic] knowledge and procedural knowledge or skills" (Nickles 1998: 78). Most importantly, schema theory aims at systematically studying *experience/perception* itself. As such, it can provide an account for the experience of chronic pain. "Once the pain schema is activated," Hardcastle writes:

> it becomes impossible not to pay attention to it, for Nature designed us to focus on our pains and decide some appropriate behavior immediately in order to ensure our survival. Chronic pain then becomes the endlessly repeated construction of a pain experience, constructed perhaps not because of some bodily trauma, but because some other stimulus input has [triggered] the loop. . . . These interactions [of brain regions within this "loop"] are felt in the experience of pain itself as a complex perceptual-emotional state as well as seen in the neuroanatomy of the brain.
>
> (1999: 119–20)

The schemas Hardcastle describes, although she does not quite say so, are "top-down," high-level structures or frameworks that organize prior

---

EXHIBIT 3.1

Thus, in speaking a language we notice and expect certain sounds and disregard aspects of those sounds that do not fit into a language schema. In English, for example, sound pitch is disregarded except in the special case of questions. Some languages, like Chinese, make the pitch of a sound something that is both explicitly attended to and expected in particular words (as native speakers of English attend to pitch and expect it to matter in questions [i.e., sentences] but not in words).

experience and help us interpret new situations. In a simple example, if we enter a strange room and find rows of chairs, colorful posters, a large desk, a "classroom schema" may help us interpret new situations (see Gureckis and Goldstone 2011); similarly, in a narrative we notice and expect certain characters to behave in certain relations with other characters. Both of these examples describe the *attention and expectation* schemas give rise to—what we notice and what we expect to notice— and there is good evidence that schemas organizing larger frameworks of cognition, such as schemas of "narrative knowledge," are evolutionarily inherited in the same way we inherit schemas of language acquisition (see Steen 2005; Schleifer and Vannatta 2013). Such schemas *condition* experience: think of the felt-anxiety children feel when they enter a room that has the "salient features" of a doctor's office.

Hardcastle describes chronic pain as essentially "weird" (1999: 69) because it exists outside pain's functions to warn of harm, reduce harmful results, and promote healing that we saw in the physiological analysis of pain: chronic pain serves no recognizable ends in terms of material (evolutionary) adaptation. In order to understand this phenomenon in material-physiological terms, she suggests that there are two neuro-logical systems associated with the *complex* phenomenon of pain, which divides "what we have been calling our pain system into two different and independent processing streams" (1999: 131). The first, "a pain sensory system (PSS)"—later she calls it "a nociceptor-driven pain sensory system" —that supports a view of pain "as a completely objective phenomena," parallel to the descriptions in the preceding chapter of nociceptive fibers, inflammation, the spine, the brain: "a PSS functions according to the same basic rules of all our sensory systems" (1999: 96; she adds that in this framework "the pain system is a simpler system than, say, vision or audition [and thus allows us] to take pain perception as a paradigm instance of a conscious experience"). This is a "bottom-up" system, beginning with *localizable* "basic" elements and rules.

The second neurological system she postulates is a "largely top-down" pain inhibitory system (or PIS) (1999: 130), which she speculates developed independently of the PSS in order to actively inhibit the pain sensation that the PSS creates, but also, oddly (given its name), to *increase* pain in certain situations. She argues that a two-system theory of pain is particularly adaptive, since it serves the material struggle for existence by keeping us informed of the status of our bodies (the function PSS) while also shutting down the pain sensation the PSS creates when flight or fight is imminent and enhancing it at other times in the service of healing. In other words, the PIS accounts for widely reported phenomena of people acting and feeling that they are *not* in pain, as when a seriously injured person might lift an automobile or flee from danger. "If our brains are geared for motor control," she concludes, "then the dual pain system makes good biological sense" (1999: 96, 134). Moreover, the existence of two parallel pain systems accounts for the more widely reported phenomena of chronic pain, with people acting and feeling that they are in great pain, without a readily available physiological ("bottom-up") cause.

In a similar fashion, Melanie Thernstrom describes "two different pain systems—one of pain perception and one of pain modulation, which involve both distinct and overlapping brain structures" (2010: 289ff.), but Hardcastle's detailed assertion that pain is a *sensory* system situates her at an extreme materialist account of pain. That is, important to her discussion is the parallel between neurological functioning of sensory systems—pain, sight, hearing—which was already described in Chapter 2. No matter how complex and, to date, still relatively obscure the sight and hearing sensory systems are—with various processing streams, little knowledge of how colors, shapes, and motions get joined in vision, etc.—she contends that "the parts of the brain that normally respond to impinging photons are part of the visual system, and the parts of the brain normally sensitive to air compression trains are part of the auditory system" (1999: 97). "Ultimately," she claims ". . . our system for perceiving pain works in exactly the same fashion as our visual and auditory systems: it is a complex [neurological] system with dissociable subsystems" (1999: 101).

Still, the pain inhibitory "subsystem" (PIS) she postulates is significantly different from the pain sensory "subsystem" (PSS)—or, for that matter, it is significantly different from dissociable subsystems in other sensory systems. It is so because in her description, it has *two* functions: it *inhibits* pain sensation, as already noted, but it also *increases* sensory phenomena in certain cases—particularly in cases of chronic pain.

It does so, she suggests, because it is a "top-down" system. Thus, evidence of a good deal of phenomena seemingly related to pain that does not produce *sensations* of pain and a good deal of pain phenomena that creates pain *sensations* (feelings) without physiological correlates suggest that some such a system of pain inhibition/excitation exists. (Grahek explicitly agrees with Hardcastle on this point: "That we can conceive injury without pain as well as pain without injury is rather to be explained by the simple fact that they are, to use traditional terminology, distinct existences" [2001: 163]). In one example of such phenomena, it was accurately reported that severely wounded soldiers during World War II did not report or exhibit symptoms of pain from their wounds (Fishman 2000: 109–10; see also Brand and Yancey 1997: 204); and another study reported that "37 percent of patients who arrived at an emergency clinic with a variety of serious injuries 'stated that they did not feel pain at the time of injury'" (cited in Grahek 2001: 161). Another powerful instance is self-injurious behavior (SIB), perhaps best exemplified by people who purposely cause themselves physical harm, such as cutting themselves or pulling their hair. The majority of such people do not feel pain during SIB (Hardcastle 1999: 123; see also 135–43). In a slightly different register where sensations of pain exist but are discounted—as in "radical frontal lobotomies [which] relieve the suffering of intractable pain, though without changing awareness of the pain itself" (Hardcastle 1999: 117)—"pain [is] still present, but it [is] a sensation rather than a threat" (Freeman and Watts 1950: 353). Finally, in Chapter 4 a number of treatments of pain are described, which are less radical than lobotomies—such as placebos, hypnosis, and other non-invasive therapies and palliative procedures—that seem to moderate pain even in the presence of injury.

Pain without Concomitant Injury: Chronic Pain as a Disease

Just as there are "situations" of pain without the experience of pain, there are many modes of experiencing pain sensation not associated with actual tissue damage. It is precisely these situations that lead Hardcastle to posit two functions of the PIS, including physiological mechanisms of pain enhancement. In *The Challenge of Pain* Melzack and Wall describe the "dissociation" of pain from injury:

(1) the relationship between pain and injury is highly variable;
(2) innocuous stimuli may produce pain; (3) the location of pain
may be different from the location of damage; (4) pain may
persist in the absence of injury or after healing.

(1983: 165)

In addition, certain drugs can cause people to wince in pain, yet they
cannot locate where the alleged pain is (Hardcastle 1999: 147).

Still, perhaps the most extreme form of chronic pain—a form that
presents in stark form the four modes of the dissociation of pain from
injury Melzack and Wall describe—is *phantom limb pain*. (The epigraph
to this chapter describes an instance of phantom limb pain.) The term
"phantom limb" was coined by the Civil War physician and novelist, Silas
Weir Mitchell (whose rest-cure inspired Charlotte Perkins Gilman's
short story "The Yellow Wallpaper"). Mitchell was a pioneer in the clinical
study of pain, which he began in relation to amputations during the Civil
War, where he found soldiers felt pain in missing limbs, though even
earlier Lord Nelson, who lost his arm in battle, declared that the fact he
could "feel" his missing fingers proved to him the existence of God. In
any case, the wide array of studies of "phantom limb pain" demonstrates
that pain is, in fact, experienced in missing or amputated parts of the
body (fingers, hands, limbs, etc.). Such pain affects upwards of two-thirds
of amputees, who often, even after fifteen years or more, still experience
"cramping and burning sensations [that] had not eased with time"
(Thernstrom 2010: 47). One study movingly describes how the very
absence of a limb often creates persistent pains that "sometimes . . . last
for decades. For example, amputees may feel the fingers of the missing
hand turned inward and digging into the palm. Absent toes seem
crampled ('bunched up'). An entire missing leg can feel icy or burning.
A nonexistent wedding ring may still supply its reassuring pressure
around a nonexistent finger" (Morris 1991: 153). Another researcher
describes a kind of "pain memory" associated with phantom pain:

some patients say that the pain they felt in their limbs immediately prior to amputation persists as a kind of pain memory.
For example, soldiers who have grenades blow up in their hands

often report that their phantom hand is in a fixed position, clenching the grenade, ready to toss it. The pain in the hand is excruciating—the same they felt the instant the grenade exploded, seared permanently in their brains.

(Ramachandran and Blakeslee 1998: 51; see also Melzack for a discussion of "pain memories," 1993: 627)

One explanation for phantom limb pain and other forms of chronic pain is what is called *chronic pain syndrome*. Later, this chapter touches upon two other explanations in relation to suggestions of a "pain sensory system" and of a putative "neuromatrix" governing the sense of a self-body image. But the notion of chronic pain syndrome can help us understand the wider phenomenon of chronic pain more clearly. In this, nerve damage itself can be understood as the cause of many instances of chronic pain. As Thernstrom notes:

the undeadness of dead nerves is at the center of the mystery of chronic pain—the ghost ringing the church bell in the empty steeple, signaling destruction on the land. Much chronic pain is now understood to be neuropathic—a pathology of the nervous system originating either in damage to the central nervous system of the brain and spinal cord or in damage to peripheral sensory nerves.

(2010: 138)

Thernstrom goes on to suggest that "the body's pain system is not hardwired, but soft-wired (what neuroscientists call 'plastic'), and it can be maladaptively molded by pain to increase its pain sensitivity" either in terms of *peripheral sensitization* or *central sensitization* (2010: 138). There is some disagreement concerning whether phantom limb pain is a phenomenon of the peripheral nerves, the spinal cord, or the brain (for these different "locations" of phantom pain see Wall 1999: 108, Vertosick 2000: 46, Glucklich 2001: 54–57), but there is no controversy concerning the empirical fact that such pain occurs. Thernstrom concludes with this sad generalization:

pain begets pain. The longer that pain pathways relay pain messages, the more efficient those pathways become, causing greater pain to be transmitted, the way a stream carves a path through land, so that over time, it flows more quickly and turns into a river.

(2010: 139)

It is this very long-time existence that defines chronic pain as a disease. (See Exhibit 3.2)

Pain as Sensation

The phenomenon of the experience/perception of pain without a clear connection to tissue damage is often the problem of chronic pain as a disease, a phenomenon detailed more fully in Chapter 5. This phenomenon leads to two explanations: for Hardcastle it suggests that pain is best understood in relation to a neurological sensory system; for Ronald

---

EXHIBIT 3.2

In discussing the enormous amount of pain-relief medicine consumed in the United States, Paul Brand suggests another account for the existence of chronic pain syndrome. He notes that "the emergence of 'chronic pain syndrome,' a phenomenon rarely seen in non-Western countries or in medical literature from the past, should set off alarms for a culture committed to painlessness" (1997: 189). Brand goes on to note that this syndrome may be a result of the body's desire to conserve energy: just as muscles that are not used atrophy, so he argues, "some researchers believe that an addiction to painrelieving medications may have a similar effect on the brain. If we suppress the need for brain endorphins (the body's natural painkillers) by providing artificial substitutes, the brain may 'forget how' to produce the natural substances. Heroin addicts show the final result: an addict's brain demands more and more artificial substances because it can no longer satisfy the cravings of its own opiate receptor sites. Long-term heroin addicts sometimes develop hypersensitivity to pain after they come off the drug. The slightest pressure of a sheet or clothing causes intense pain because the brain no longer manufactures the neurotransmitters that deal with such routine stimuli" (1997: 189). In Chapter 4, the functioning of opioid pain killers, which include heroin, is examined.

Melzack (as we see in the next section) it suggests that pain is best understood in terms of a neurological cognitive system. Thus, Hardcastle notes that "parallels between pain illusions and our other [sensory] systems" help define the *complexity* of fact/event and experience/perception of pain described throughout this book. Thus she describes a common phenomenon of visual processing:

> we see a straight stick as bent when placed halfway in water. . . . We make these perceptual errors because, either through learning from experience or by design, our brains develop shortcuts [by which she means the top-down cognitive shortcuts of *schemas*] in computing our percepts that inevitably fail us under certain conditions. . . . Similarly, our pain system may be designed to operate efficiently but inaccurately.
>
> (1999: 127)

Still, she notes that "what is interesting and different [from other sensory systems] about our pains is the PIS. It is geared to suppress or enhance the activity of a single sensory system, and there is no other system quite like it in our nervous system" (1999: 145–46). "We cannot hear a loud noise," she notes,

> without also hearing that noise at some pitch. If a brain is not given some of the information regarding the structure of an object or a sound, then it simply fills in what is missing.
>
> In distinction, pain sensations function quite differently. We quite often get one aspect of pain [such as its "bodily location, somatic quality, a feeling of suffering, a negative reaction we call 'pain'"] without the others. Moreover, if we are lacking an aspect—say, we have the somatic quality without the suffering or negative reaction—then our brains feel no obligation to fill in the missing pieces.
>
> (1999: 151)

The uniqueness of pain, for Hardcastle—and for most pain research as well—is that the pain sensory system is both like and unlike other sensory systems. (See Exhibit 3.3.) That is, like other systems of sensation or perception—her examples are almost exclusively sight and hearing, but one could add taste and smell as well (Brand nicely focuses on taste when contrasting pain and pleasure (1997: 295–296))—pains are normal (insofar as normally functioning creatures have them), natural, commonplace, and seem to give information about the external environment. The problem, however, is that quite often pains *do not seem to give information about the external environment*, and Hardcastle suggests that they *never do* (1999: 129–30). She does suggest that dreams might be similar phenomena, "but," she adds, "unlike with dreams, we do not realize when a pain is over that it really was not about the external world after all" (1999: 130).

Although she rarely talks about the olfactory sensory system and never describes taste, the most important sensory system she also fails to mention is touch. Touch, as the description of nociceptor receptors suggested in Chapter 2, is closely related to the sensory system of pain: after all touch is associated with the A-beta fibers that are sensitive to gentle pressure. In *The Body in Pain*, Elaine Scarry offers a wonderful description of touch as distinct from pain. She writes:

> If a thorn cuts through the skin of [a] woman's finger, she feels not the thorn but her body hurting her. If instead she experiences across the skin of her fingers not the awareness of the feel of those fingers but the feel of the fine weave of another woman's work, . . . she . . . experiences the sensation of 'touch' not as bodily sensations but as self-displacing, self-transforming objectification.
>
> (1985: 166)

EXHIBIT 3.3

Paul Brand notes that "pain is unique among sensations. Other senses tend to habituate, or lessen over time; the strongest cheeses seem virtually odorless after eight minutes; touch sensors adjust quickly to coarse clothing; an absent-minded professor searches in vain for his glasses, no longer feeling their weight on his head. In contrast, pain sensors do not habituate, but report incessantly to the conscious brain as long as danger remains" (1997: 217).

Scarry goes on to argue that this feeling is called "pleasure"—an issue taken up towards the end of this book. "Pleasure," she says, is "a word usually reserved either for moments of overt disembodiment or, as here, moments when acute bodily sensations are experienced as something other than one's own body" (1985: 166). In a note to this passage, she further describes pleasure as "a condition associated with living beyond the physical body, or experiencing bodily sensations in terms of objectified content" (1985: 355). Pain, as it has been described in this and the preceding chapter in terms of its physiology and concomitant affect (i.e., its experience), is a condition associated with living *completely within* the physical body insofar as, Marcel Proust said, it makes one "deaf and blind to other people, to life, to everything except my wretched body" (Daudet 2002: 15).

Pain and Cognition

Very different from an understanding of pain as a neurological sensory system parallel to sight and hearing is a model developed by Melzack that relates the experience/perception of pain to the cognition of the person as a "self" in an elaborate "neuromatrix theory" that attempts to make sense of the phantom limb pain mentioned earlier, and the even odder phenomenon of phantom pain felt in absent limbs by people who were born without those limbs. Basing his surmise in large part on this curious latter phenomenon, Melzack postulates a "body-self template" that provides "the neuropsychological foundation of the phenomenal self" (Glucklich 2001: 58; by "phenomenal self" Glucklich means the felt-experience of being a unique individual). "The anatomical substrate of the body-self," Melzack writes, ". . . is a large, widespread network of neurons that consists of loops between the thalamus and cortex as well as between the cortex and limbic system" (1993: 621). Marni Jackson glosses Melzack's theory: "The concept of a neuromatrix," she writes, "suggests that pain is not an invasive, alien force or a learned response but part of the map of who we are" (2002: 76). What is most striking about Melzack's theory of a neuromatrix is that he is positing a theory of the experience of "selfhood" on the basis of the experience of pain. In an early articulation of his theory, he argues that the phantom limb pain creates "new avenues of the understanding of the self, the mind, and reality" (1989: 2); and he goes on to say that it is precisely "*the quality of pain experiences*" that is the key to a neurological understanding the experience of selfhood: such "*pain experiences* must not be confused with the physical event of breaking skin or bone" (1989: 9). He concludes by asserting, on the basis of the phenomenon of phantom limb pain, that "phantoms become comprehensible once we recognize that the brain generates the experience of the body" (1993: 628). Melzack's neuromatrix:

> is a neural network that is laid down early in the developing embryo to prepare the brain for a certain set of responses it can expect to use. For instance, at birth the brain already 'knows' and 'feels' a body with two legs, even if the child is born with one leg missing.
>
> (Jackson 2002: 328)

In this, Melzack's theory of a neuromatrix gives rise to cognitive rather than a sensory apprehension.

In light of Melzack's assertion that the brain generates the experience of the body, Hardcastle's contention that he is reinstating a mind–body dichotomy seems plausible. But such a dichotomy itself seems a function of the opposition between the fact/event of pain and the experience/perception of pain. This is why I am inclined to agree with Hardcastle's notion that if we focus on *schemas* of pain experience, resulting from the material organization of the brain (whether inherited or nurtured in post-natal brain development [see Edelman 2005]), the opposition of fact and experience is no longer crucial insofar as the schemas of experience might well be "localizable" in neurological facts/events. Moreover, we can understand Melzack's theory of a neuromatrix— including his sense that "the repeated *cyclical processing and synthesis* of nerve impulses through the neuromatrix imparts a characteristic pattern: the *neurosignature*," which creates the *cognitive* perception of a "body-self" (1989: 8)—as itself an elaborately detailed material localization of a neurological *schema*. That is, Melzack argues that "heredity and environment together influence the signature pattern" (1989: 8), and his speculation of a "matrix" of repeated nerve impulses might very well offer an outline for how neurological schemas of cognition and experience physiologically organize themselves.

In this understanding, the opposition of understanding the nature of pain either as *sensory* (a physiological fact/event) or as *perceptive* (a cognitive/emotional experience) no longer seems a crucial opposition. Pain, as the discussions of the physiological and phenomenal nature of pain in these two chapters have demonstrated, is a *complex* of "the elusive intersection of three overlapping circles—cognition, sensation, and emotion" (Thernstrom 2010: 284), and as such the phenomenon of human pain integrates scientific fact and individual/cultural experience. In fact, Melzack himself has stated that "what [the neuromatrix] concept incorporates is that culture is not 'out there,' but something integrated into all the patterns of thinking in our mind" (cited in Jackson 2002: 334). The final chapter in Part I, "The Nature of Pain," focusing on treating pain, should make this complex understanding of pain particularly clear insofar as it examines pharmaceutical, cultural, and psychological ways of treating and relieving the complex fact/experience of pain in human life. Part II presents a more thorough examination of individual and cultural experiences of pain.

Treating Pain: Operations, Drug Therapy, Placebos, and Palliative Care

"What would you say is the earliest sign of civilization," [the anthropologist Margaret Mead] asked, naming a few options. A clay pot? Tools made of iron? The first domesticated plants? "These are all early signs," she continued, "but here is what I believe to be evidence of the earliest signs of civilization." High above her head she held a human femur, the largest bone in the leg, and pointed to a grossly thickened area where the bone had been fractured, and then solidly healed. "Such signs of healing are never found among the remains of the earliest, fiercest societies. In their skeletons we find clues of violence: a rib pierced by an arrow, a skull crushed by a club. But this healed bone shows that someone must have cared for the injured person— hunted on his behalf, brought him food, served him at personal sacrifice."

With Margaret Mead, I believe that this quality of shared pain is central to what it means to be a human being.

—Dr. Paul Brand, *The Gift of Pain*
(Brand and Yancey 1997: 274–75)

From time immemorial human beings have helped one another to relieve or cope with pain. As Margaret Mead suggests, such care in the face of

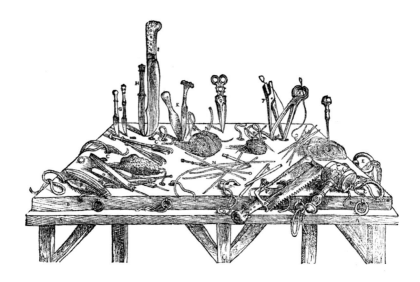

Figure 4.1 Treating Pain

human suffering might well be the best indication of civilized human life. Many potions were discovered and used in the most ancient of times all over the world: cannabis (which Herodotus notes caused "the wounded Scythians to howl with relief and joy"); henbane (used in witches' brew); mandrake root (a plant that was said to shriek in pain when uprooted, yet could be made into a medicine to ease pain); cocaine (the only ancient remedy used in surgery: "the ancient Incas used the leaves of the sacred coca plant to perform operations"); and most of all opium (the ancient Sumerians' "plant of joy")—all of which seem to have preceded wine and distilled spirits as antidotes to pain (see Thernstrom 2010: 48ff.; 104, 102). "A person on opiates," Melanie Thernstrom has written:

> seems to have all his senses about him—he can still run a marathon and will still cry out in pain if he falls and hurts himself—yet his relationship to pain is strangely altered. In addition to blocking the transmission of pain signals, opiates . . . change one's relation to pain, so that the pain no longer

preys on one's mind. This more complicated effect may be due to the way in which opiates boost the level of dopamine in the brain, creating a sense of pleasantness or even euphoria.

(2010: 104)

Thus, from ancient times up until the nineteenth century many pain remedies were various combinations of opium and alcohol; ancient Egyptian tablets from before Christ depict an operation that includes pressure to compress the nerves of a patient's arm; evidence dating from the Shang Dynasty (1600–1100 BCE) suggests that acupuncture was practiced in very ancient times; more recently, during the Napoleonic wars at the turn of the nineteenth century, limbs were frozen before amputation (Fishman 2000: 30); and about the same time "mesmerism"— coined from the practice of the Austrian physician, Dr. Anton Mesmer, in the late eighteenth century—introduced hypnosis as a remedy for pain and an anesthetic for surgery. In addition, from ancient times there were operations to relieve pain (such as trepanation, the creation of a hole in the skull to relieve pain, evidence for which has been widely found in prehistoric remains), as well as non-invasive strategies of religious medi-tation, prayer, and caretaking and palliative care. These ancient treat-ments for pain—invasive therapies (such as surgical operations), drug therapies (including attempted anesthetics), non-invasive therapies (such as exercise, meditation, etc.), and systematic palliative care (such as religious hospices)—all remain as methods of addressing pain in human civilizations in our time. In fact, Dr. Frank Vertosick notes that today we "have three broad ways of treating any chronic pain: (1) eliminate the underlying cause; (2) treat the pain itself; or (3) alter the psychological perception of pain," and he goes on to suggest that the strategies work best in this order (2000: 255). These antidotes to pain, both ancient and modern, along with the physiology of acute pain and the phenomenon of chronic pain, help to delineate the nature of pain as both fact/event and perception/experience.

Surgical Therapies

Perhaps the most obvious "physiological" treatment of chronic pain is to remove that part of the body that is the source of such pain. However, such surgery (called "ablative surgery") has proved to create only temporary relief. In most cases, pain returns within a year. The phenomenon of phantom limb pain resulting from amputation, discussed in Chapter 3, is an instance of chronic pain *resulting* from a surgical operation, but Valerie Gray Hardcastle suggests another way of thinking about the weak results of ablative surgery. She notes that the spinothalamic pain tract—the pain transmission system between peripheral nerves, the dorsal horn, and the brain discussed in Chapter 2—is "a relatively young system, appearing in higher primates but not in the lower primates," and notes that surgical incisions in similar areas of this tract in higher primates do not give consistent results in terms of pain relief (1999: 175). The consequences of these facts are two-fold. First of all, one consequence is that there can be little animal testing of surgical techniques to relieve pain. But in addition, the fact that animals without the spinothalamic tract still have pain suggests that alternative, more primitive paths of pain transmission exist alongside the spinothalamic tract in humans. Hardcastle notes that:

> in most cases of evolution, when something new comes on the scene, it overlays what was there previously; it does not replace it. Therefore, it stands to reason that we too have some phylogenetically older pain signal systems. Oblating all these systems in the correct place is difficult to do, especially since we don't know exactly where they are.
>
> (1999: 176)

Whether or not this explanation is correct—after all, Chapter 2 presented pain sources at least partially outside the spinothalamic tract such as inflammation, which, I note later in this chapter, is the object of many analgesic pain relievers—the fact remains that ablative surgery is relatively rare and, also, it is usually ineffective over the long term. There remain some ablative surgeries for neurological conditions such as Parkinson's disease, but surgery has proven a relatively poor treatment for relief of chronic pain. David Morris even observes that "some operations once commonly used for chronic pain actually left 15 percent of the patients with *worse* pain" (1991: 70).

Still, the most dramatic operation for pain relief in the twentieth century was the lobotomy, an operation that won the physician who developed it, António Egas Moniz, the Nobel Prize in 1949. The prefrontal lobotomy—an operation (sometimes called leucotomy) that severs nerve fibers that connect the prefrontal lobe to other areas of the brain—was initially developed to "calm" disturbed people, usually performed to treat patients' mental illnesses of one form or another. But it was also used throughout the mid-twentieth century (1930s–1950s) to relieve chronic pain. It was found that radical frontal lobotomies relieve intractable pain without changing the awareness (sensation?) of the pain itself (see Exhibit 4.1). Grahek uses the phenomenon of the dissociation of the sensation of pain from its feeling of distress—it is sometimes called "extreme reactive dissociation syndrome"—to question whether the sensation of pain is all there is of pain, or whether the phenomenon of pain *requires* (as I have suggested in Chapter 3 that it does) a cognitive as well as a sensory component. "A complete indifference to pain," he argues:

> would also mean that one is not at all distressed by pain; that pain is no longer the object of anxiety, fear, or dread; that pain does not signify threat or danger; and, finally, what is hardest to understand, that pain is no longer disliked or experienced as inherently unpleasant. Such indifference to pain would actually mean that the emotional-cognitive and behavioral components of pain experience would be dissociated from its sensory-discriminative components: that one would be able to feel pain,

---

EXHIBIT 4.1

Walter Jackson Freeman and James W. Watts note that "Lobotomy does not . . . abolish the normal reaction to pain. It does reduce the persistent, obsessive, emotional substrate of continued pain. We would compare this situation with the dynamite charge that is detonated by a percussion cup. The emotional substrate represents the explosive, and when this is removed, the percussion cup can go off any number of times without resulting in a great explosion" (1950: 372).

localize it, determine its intensity and qualitative character, and yet not react to it in any way. If that is possible, it would be a case of a radical reactive dissociation syndrome in human pain experience.

(2001: 31)

Dr. Paul Brand narrates a vivid example of a woman who had a lobotomy to relieve intractable pain: when he asked her about her pain, she said, "'Oh, yes, it's still there. I just don't worry about it anymore.' She smiled sweetly and chuckled to herself. 'In fact, it's still agonizing. But I don't mind'" (Brand and Yancey 1997: 210). Still, after the 1950s, surgeons became reluctant to perform lobotomy because it was found that it had far-reaching effects on personality, creating in patients intense apathy, passivity, lack of initiative, poor ability to concentrate, and a generally decreased depth and intensity of their emotional response to life ("Lobotomy," *Encyclopedia Britannica*). (See Exhibit 4.2.)

Drug Therapies

Anesthesia

Perhaps the most important—surely the most dramatic—therapy for pain was the development of general anesthesia to allow for relatively painless surgery. (Surgical pain is by definition an example of acute pain, although as we saw in the case of phantom limb pain, surgery can also lead to chronic pain. On occasion, surgery can also provoke chronic pain syndrome, as occurred in the experience of Reynolds Price discussed later in this chapter.) It wasn't until 1846 that a general anesthetic was

---

EXHIBIT 4.2

More than a century ago, in *Functions of the Brain*, David Ferrier noted that "an animal deprived of its frontal lobes retains all its power of voluntary motion unimpaired and that it continues to see, hear, smell and taste and to perceive and localize tactile impressions as before. . . . And yet, . . . [the animals] generally appear to have lost the faculty of intelligent and attentive observation" (1886: 231–32).

successfully used in a public surgery demonstration at Harvard University in an operating theater known, since then, as the "ether dome." Before that time, necessary operations were done without anesthetics: in fact the great poet, John Keats, trained to be a surgeon in the early nineteenth century, and part of his work was to help hold down patients as surgery was performed. In 1812 the novelist, Fanny Burney, wrote a powerful narrative of her mastectomy without anesthetics. David Morris vividly summarizes her experience:

> With a passion for exactness, Burney records every detail of this brutal operation. She describes the knife plunged into her breast, "cutting through veins—arteries—flesh—nerves." She describes the air rushing into the wound like a mass of "sharp & forked poniards"—the surgeon "cutting against the grain" . . . Modern readers will find it hard to forget the scream that she says lasted uninterruptedly during the entire time of the incision. "I almost marvel that it rings not in my Ears still!" she wrote afterward: "so excruciating was the agony."
>
> (1991: 63)

This operation took place in Burney's house: the surgeons arrived with little warning since at that time surgeons would not schedule a precise day for surgery for fear that patients would commit suicide to avoid the agony of an operation (Thernstrom 2010: 97).

In fact, until 1846, there was no way to remove tumors (such as Fanny Burney's), amputate gangrenous limbs, or repair internal damage without inflicting horrendous pain. Yet several years before Burney's surgery in the early nineteenth century, Sir Humphrey Davy discovered the anesthetic properties of nitrous oxide. But there was strong opposition from the medical profession to anesthetics: it was felt that avoiding pain was blasphemously resisting God's will for humankind, and many thought, as the Scottish surgeon Sir Charles Bell argued in 1806, that pain is "necessary to our existence" (cited in Thernstrom 2010: 110). In fact, it was not until almost a half century after the discovery of the anesthetic properties of nitrous oxide that anesthetics were medically applied, at first in dentistry. (Dentistry, unlike most medical surgeries, did not treat a life-threatening condition, and dentists needed pain relief to encourage patients to take their services.) A young dentist, William Morton, convinced a well-known surgeon at Massachusetts General Hospital, Dr. John Warren, to use ether during surgery, and in October 1846 a young man had a tumor of his jaw removed without pain in the famous demonstration in the ether dome. One surgeon present at the operation declared that "our craft has, once and for all, been robbed of its terrors" (cited in Fishman 2000: 28).

Despite initial reservations from some surgeons, by the end of the nineteenth century, biological understanding of pain—that is to say, the understanding of pain as a fact and/or an event—superseded the religious understandings of pain and suffering:

> by the end of the Victorian era, the underlying debate was conclusively settled: there was no meaning to pain. Pain was not a metaphor; it was a biological by-product of disease. The body had been claimed as the province of science, the patient dispossessed. Pain was not passion, alchemy, ordeal . . . acute surgical pain could be controlled by anesthesia.
>
> (Thernstrom 2010: 120)

Moreover, the results were palpable: in the middle of the century, before anesthesia, average life expectancy in the United States and western Europe was approximately thirty-five years; as general anesthesia was more and more widely used, life increased until anyone born around 1900, Dr. Scott Fishman notes, could expect to live to more than fifty (2000: 29)—though I must add dramatic increases in public health (e.g., sanitation, clean water supplies, the germ theory of disease, etc.) were at least equally instrumental in increasing life expectancy.

Anesthetics function by inducing a temporary inability to perceive sensory stimuli, primarily touch, pressure, and pain. In other words, general anesthetics render patients unconscious. The difficulty is controlling such unconsciousness: in an early attempt to demonstrate "painless dentistry" a Harford dentist, Horace Wells, organized a demonstration of nitrous oxide (again with Dr. Warren) a year before the 1846 operation, but the amount of gas was inadequate and the patient screamed in pain (Vertosick 2000: 200). But even worse, too often patients would not come out of unconsciousness and died because of the anesthesia (especially early uses of chloroform). In the twentieth century, anesthesiologists developed an array of anesthesia-inducing substances and procedures to render them safe and effective, "monitoring the patient's condition breath by breath so that anyone, from early premature babies to centenarians, can be assured of safe anaesthesia" (Wall 1999: 199). In the twenty-first century, anesthesiologists administer hundreds of drugs: "drugs to induce sleep, to induce paralysis, to raise and lower blood pressure, to ease pain, to raise and lower heart rate, to correct aberrant heart rhythms, to regulate blood sugar, to increase urine output, and so on" (Vertosick 2000: 209). General anesthesia, as Dr. Frank Vertosick notes, "ranks high among the greatest achievements of our age" (2000: 210).

As well as general anesthesia, there are a host of local anesthetics. In fact, Sigmund Freud was a powerful early researcher into local anesthetics, which were pursued since they avoided early dangers—often mortal—of general anesthesia (Fishman 2000: 36). Freud was particularly interested in cocaine, which he discovered functions as a local anesthetic (it is still sometimes used in eye surgery). But cocaine has a long history: the ancient Incans used it for trepanation, and the Spanish conquistadores used it as well: they found its qualities for both energizing people and suppressing appetite were a "useful addition for the slaves" (Thernstrom 2010: 104). It is likely that cocaine's ability to create euphoria and suppress appetite stems from its interaction with neurotransmitters such as norephinephrine and dopamine. Cocaine is highly addictive, but in the early twentieth century chemists synthesized related substances that numb local areas without creating euphoria. They labeled this group of chemicals "procaine," which is also distributed under the name of "Novocain" (Fishman 2000: 37–38).

Analgesics

Unlike anesthetics, analgesics are drugs that relieve pain without affecting consciousness or sensory perception. There are two types of analgesic drugs: anti-inflammatory drugs that alleviate pain by reducing local inflammation; and the opioids, which act on the brain and the central nervous system. Anti-inflammatory drugs are used for short-term pain relief for such conditions as headaches, muscle strain, arthritis. Opioid analgesics are used for relief of severe pain (both short term and long term). The most widely known anti-inflammatory is aspirin—a trade name for acetylsalicylic acid—that is a derivative of salicylic acid. Aspirin was marketed by Friedrich Bayer and Company in the 1890s—it was the first "block buster" pharmaceutical that commanded worldwide sales. Although aspirin has been remarkably effective, it was not until recently that the physiological basis of its effects were discovered: aspirin acts by inhibiting the production of prostaglandins, body chemicals that are necessary for blood clotting and are noted for sensitizing nerve endings to pain. Around 1960 the FDA approved a new anti-inflammatory, acetaminophen, marketed under the brand name Tylenol. Unlike aspirin, Tylenol does not create irritation of the stomach and gastrointestinal tract. Still, the most common cause of acute liver failure in the west is toxicity from acetaminophen, and the vast majority of people suffering from this condition in the United States are women (Thernstrom 2010: 147; see also Fishman 2000: 41).

Like analgesics, opioids also relieve pain without affecting consciousness or sensory perception. Opioid is the term for both natural opiates derived from the opium poppy and similar synthesized chemical compounds (e.g., methadone). Natural opiates such as opium have been used since ancient times: some scholars think Odysseus encounters opium in Homer's *Odyssey*, and the great medieval physician Paracelsus is said to have mixed opium with alcohol to produce laudanum, used through the nineteenth century to control pain. Both opium and laudanum produce sleep and vivid dreams, and the poet Samuel Taylor Coleridge claimed to have written his great poem "Kubla Khan" under the influence of laudanum. Derivatives of opium, namely morphine and heroin, produce such psychedelic effects—heroin was developed (by Bayer) in the early twentieth century, and morphine and a weaker derivative, codeine, were used in medicine since about that time—but in the twentieth century low doses of opioids were seen to produce purely analgesic effects while leaving patients thinking clearly.

Unlike the anti-inflammatory drugs, opioids act on the central nervous system, and in fact in 1976 it was discovered that the body naturally produces substances similar in chemical structure to morphine that dampen pain and enhance pleasure. That is, in the early 1970s scientists found opiate receptors in the brain cells of mice, and soon after neuro-peptides related to these receptors were found that function in human beings as neuromodulators in the nervous system and as hormones in the endocrine system. Such neuropeptides modulate pain, mood, sleep, sedation, and coughing at opiate receptor sites by inhibiting the regen-eration of nerve impulses. These substances were shown to be natural products of the human body, and at first they were called "endorphins," from the combination of Greek terms meaning "produced in the body" and "morphine." Now we know there are three kinds of natural opioids—endorphins, enkephalins, and dynorphins—but "endorphin" has become the term describing them all (Fishman 2000: 119). Endorphin receptors have also been found in the glands, the intestines, the stomach, and in the central nervous system as well as the brain. Fishman notes that:

> evidence that endorphins suppress the body's production of Substance P, a chemical that washes through damaged and inflamed tissue, may explain why morphine injected into inflamed joints provides long-acting pain relief and how endorphins can mute other types of pain. A major place where endorphins circulate is the pituitary gland, which may partly explain how exertion and exercise can change pain and even produce moods like "runner's high." There are also opioid receptors in the sex glands, and . . . animal studies [report] endorphin levels jump 200 percent between arousal and orgasm.
>
> (2000: 119–20)

Endorphins, then, are pain inhibitors produced by the human body, and, with other opioids, both natural and synthesized, they function to reduce inflammation as well as inhibit pain. There is also good evidence that they are connected with "pleasure centers" in the brain, which include subcortical regions (such as the nucleus accumbens and ventral pallidum) and cortical regions (orbitofrontal cortex and anterior cingulate cortex) (see Kringlebach 2008).

They also function to create addiction of one sort or another. This is of great importance, because in part the addictive nature of opioids has led to their significant under-utilization in the treatment of pain. Opioids possess the potential to create "tolerance"—the ability to absorb and require larger and larger doses—and physical dependence. That is, like well-known members of the opioid family such as heroin and morphine, they challenge the body's resources such that the body makes biochemical, physiological, and psychological readjustment to tolerate and accommodate their effects. At this point, the cellular response has so altered itself as to require the continued presence of the drug to maintain normal function—this is what is meant by "physical dependence." When the substance is abruptly withdrawn, the cellular response becomes abnormal for a time until a new readjustment is made (Steiner 2013). This kind of physical addiction has led physicians to exhibit great reluctance to prescribe opioids, even in the face of significant chronic and acute pain. Moreover, it has led patients to avoid pain-reducing therapies: a study of breast cancer patients showed that the second most prevalent reason for not pursuing the pain relief of opioids was patients' fear of addiction (Thernstrom 2010: 152; the first was physician failure to recommend pain therapies). In Chapter 7, I describe a "functional" definition of addiction rather than the physiological definition presented here.

The reluctance to prescribe and use opioids is important because many have argued—especially in the 1990s—that there is good evidence that opioids administered properly do not lead to addiction; and also because in the case of pain associated with terminal diseases such concerns seem misdirected. Thus Paul Brand notes that "a drug like opium or morphine does not usually produce hallucinatory effects if taken for the relief of pain" and that "narcotics given for pain treatment do not normally result in addiction" (Brand and Yancey 1997: 249). Still, more recent studies contradict this judgment. A very recent study, *A World of Hurt* by Barry Meier (2013), chronicles the "War on Pain" campaign initiated in the late 1990s by pain experts and pharmaceutical companies. This study records very different conclusions about the use of opioid pain medicine, especially OxyContin (whose active ingredient is oxycodone). It notes that:

> the federal Centers for Disease Controls and Prevention [in the United States] recently declared that overdose deaths involving

painkillers are at "epidemic" levels: about 15,000 people die this way every year [in the United States], second to the number killed in car accidents.

(2013: loc 63)

Meier argues that "instead of helping patients resume active lives, the widespread use of these drugs, experts say, has created a nationwide legion of listless, narcotized zombies" and that "long-term use of prescription narcotics is often not an effective way to treat pain and may even worsen such conditions" (2013: loc 80, 85). Moreover, he points out that some evidence suggests that "ever-increasing dosages to overcome 'tolerance' might fundamentally alter the neurological system and make a patient hypersensitive to pain" (2013: loc 118).

Still, Meier notes that "experts say that many patients are helped by daily regimens of the drugs, particularly when used at moderate doses. And there is a small group of patients, often people suffering from rare conditions associated with excruciating pain, who need high doses" (2013: loc 336–41). Moreover, in another recent study aimed at the clinical treatment of pain, *Listening to Pain* (2012)—written by a pain physician rather than a journalist—Dr. Scott Fishman notes the usefulness of opioids (while acknowledging the dangers) in the treatment of pain. In his work, as noted in Chapter 7 in this book, he offers a "functional" rather than an essentialist definition of addiction. While the addictive dangers of opioids are real and can be seriously destructive to the quality of every-day experience and even life itself for those who do not have the "ability to control or modulate their use of a drug [to the point that it] is causing them dysfunction," the utilization of proven pain relievers that allow people who are suffering with horrible distress, often alone, to "cope" with their situation and, in fact, recover at least some desired life-functions should not be too quickly dismissed (Fishman 2012: 45–46). The judgment of proper uses of pharmaceutical pain relief leads to important *action* in the face of terrible pain. Chapter 7 returns to this issue and, following Fishman, suggests that "functional" rather than "essential" understandings of pain and addiction will allow people faced with pain—healthcare workers, companions, pain sufferers themselves—to find ways to make compassionate judgments to pursue actions that balance danger and relief.

The Placebo Effect

Another response to pain, very different from the invasion treatments of surgery and of natural and chemical drugs, is the administration of placebos to create the placebo effect. The placebo effect has been defined, somewhat technically, as the "psychological or psychophysiological improvement attributed to therapy with an inert substance or a simulated (sham) procedure" (Rogers 2013; I say "somewhat technically" because the term "psychophysiological" technically describes the combination of fact/event and perception/experience found in pain described throughout this book). It is now thought by many that the placebo effect may involve the stimulation of natural opioids such as endorphins. Whether or not this is accurate, there is substantial evidence for the reality of the placebo effect in treating pain. The term *placebo* comes from the Latin for "I shall please," and it describes inert substances (i.e., "sham" medications) that produce *effects* of *proven* medications. The phrase "sham medications" describes the administration of a sugar pill, saline solution, or more traditional treatments, such as distillations of "frogs, worms, feathers, hair, horns, hoofs, ants, scorpions, viper flesh, crab eyes, bee glue, fox lung, spider webs, teeth, sexual organs, and so forth" (Benedetti 2008: 2) for which there are no scientific demonstrations of their interaction with pain and other conditions that they nevertheless relieve. Thus about 35 percent of cancer patients report substantial relief from placebo treatment (e.g., from a saline solution they are told is a pain-relief substance such as morphine), which is about half of those who find relief from morphine itself. Moreover, the *kind* of treatment matters: in one experiment with cancer patients placebo pills created 30 percent relief, placebo injections created 40 percent relief, and intravenous placebo drip created 50 percent relief; and it has also been demonstrated that the colors of pills consistently affect their effectiveness. Finally, it is notable that some patients even grow addicted to placebos and undergo withdrawal symptoms (Brand and Yancey 1997: 211). In addition to the effectiveness of placebos, researchers have found a *measurable difference* in the positive effects of *proven* pain relievers between patients who were told they were receiving the medication and patients who were given the medication without being told. All these results suggest that a placebo effect is the explanation for many traditional methods of "cure," such as ritual scarification, chanting, meditation, and other such things (perhaps including the hypnosis and acupuncture discussed below).

Still, there is great skepticism concerning the placebo effect, particularly in those who subscribe to a strict sense of *nomological* (or "law-like") science (see Appendix I for a discussion of this term) that depends on precise measurement, blind trials, and the like. Thus, it is often noted that there is little evidence that placebos affect diseases; there is only evidence that they affect pain associated with disease. Such an attitude subscribes to the simple idea that pain cannot be a disease on its own account, but only a symptom (e.g., an "alarm") of another, overriding condition. Melanie Thernstrom addresses this skepticism and notes that:

> placebo is popularly understood as requiring some kind of sham treatment, like a sugar pill. But because the placebo effect is a result of the power of belief, or positive expectation, it can be created through verbal assurances or healing rituals as powerfully as through sham pills or procedures. Neuroimaging studies show that a placebo activates the brain's pain-modulatory system in a way that is *neurochemically indistinguishable from treatment with an opioid analgesic.*
>
> (2010: 292)

And she goes on to note that:

> even opiate medications require the placebo effect for part of their effectiveness. Studies have found that when morphine or other strong opioids are administered covertly (say, added to an IV), they don't work nearly as well as when subjects know they are receiving them. The use of a placebo increases morphine's efficacy by more than a third.
>
> (2010: 292; see Exhibit 4.3)

See Exhibit 4.3. Patrick Wall also describes the placebo effect in non-human animals: in the chapter on "The Placebo Response" in his book *Pain: The Science of Suffering* he cites a number of animal experiments

---

EXHIBIT 4.3

Melanie Thernstrom notes that "placebo has a nasty twin: nocebo (Latin for 'I will harm'), the negative effects of expectation. The brain will generate pain or other adverse responses in people who believe they have been given a harmful substance, even if they haven't. A patient who is given a fake opiate may feel undesirable side effects, such as itchiness or sleepiness, along with pain relief. . . . A negative medical prognosis can also cause a fatal nocebo, as in the syndrome of patients dying soon after being told they have terminal cancer but before the malignancy develops further" (2010: 293–94).

---

in which the "expectation" of certain effects led to measurable physiological changes in the subjects:

> If a rabbit has experienced a series of small insulin injections that decrease the blood glucose and is then given a saline injection in the same conditions, the animal reacts by raising its blood glucose. The animal has learned to counteract the effects of the drug by raising its blood sugar. With a saline injection, it reacts as though it has received the insulin.
>
> (1999: 160)

In people he notes that a parallel experiment demonstrated a similar "placebo response," but when subjects were told that the injections no longer contained insulin, no placebo response was recorded. This suggests to Wall that the placebo response is not simply a Pavlovian "conditioned response" (1999: 168) but also, on some level, a cognitive response. Moreover, this leads Wall to define pain in relation to attention and expectation (i.e., what I have been describing as the work of schemas): as we have already seen, he proposes that "pain occurs as the brain is analysing the situation [that gave rise to pain] in terms of actions that might be appropriate" (1999: 169). (See Exhibit 4.4.)

As mentioned earlier, there are many who believe that the placebo effect is the result of the stimulation of the production of natural opioids in the body, that the very *perception* of a state of affairs provokes the

---

EXHIBIT 4.4

In the clinical practice of psychotherapy, there is something related to placebos called "the dodo effect." The term comes from *Alice in Wonderland* when Dodo says "everyone has won and all must have prizes." Thus Bradley Lewis notes that "empirical studies confirm with remarkable consistency that the positive effects of therapy . . . are not due to the specific interventions of the therapist. The benefits of therapy come instead from common factors of therapeutic setting. These studies suggest that the process of setting up a therapeutic relationship with a quality therapist who is kind, empathic, and experienced is much more important than the content of the specific models and theories from which the therapist works" (Lewis 2012: 98).

---

production of pain-modulating neurochemicals (for a review of studies of this phenomenon, including brain-imaging studies, see Benedetti 2008: 74–83). But "other factors, such as desire of relief and reduction of anxiety" may contribute to the placebo effect as well as possible stimulation of endorphins. That is, "placebo phenomena occur within the context of emotional regulation, and symptoms should be influenced by desire, expectation, and intensity of emotional feeling" suggesting that "desire and expectation interact and underlie common human emotions like sadness, anxiety, and relief" (Benedetti 2008: 71; citing Price et al. 1985; Price and Barrell 2000; Price et al. 2001; Price et al. 2008). Chapter 5 touches upon these emotions of sadness and anxiety—with the addition of anger—to describe ways in which the experience of pain is exacerbated and therefore ways in which clinicians can develop strategies, beyond the drugs, placebos, and other strategies described in the current chapter, to treat pain. Note that the discussion cited above, Fabrizio Benedetti's scholarly study *Placebo Effects*, focuses on symptoms rather than disease: here again is an instance where the strict demarcation of symptom and disease, like that of Hemingway's doctor dismissing the screams of pain of his patient as "not important" (1970: 17), leads to the strict separation of experience and fact—the separation of the focuses of cultural studies and the "law-like" sciences described in Appendix I— that often impede the full treatment of pain in suffering patients.

As mentioned in the preceding chapter—and, indeed, throughout this book—the fact *and* experience of chronic pain as both symptom and disease make this way of looking at the world a problem in the understanding and treatment of pain.

Acupuncture and Hypnosis

Two procedures of pain relief present different pain treatments that might well be understood in relation to the placebo effect. The first, acupuncture, seems to stimulate natural opioid production (Han 2004); while the second, hypnosis, does not seem to stimulate such production (Hardcastle 1999: 186; among others, she cites Barber and Mayer 1977, Olness, Wain, and Lorenze 1980, Domangue et al. 1985, Spiegel and Albert 1985). Acupuncture is a treatment for pain relief that has demonstrable success without a clear and precise physiological explanation. Acupuncture is an ancient Chinese technique for relieving pain, curing disease, and promoting general health—it was developed well before 2500 BCE—and in the 1990s the Federal Drug Administration in the United States declared that acupuncture needles were no longer experimental devices. Acupuncture consists of inserting small needles through the skin into underlying tissue usually less than half an inch deep at precise points of the human body. (There are elaborate acupuncture maps describing positions of insertion.) It is consistently effective in relieving pain, and is sometimes used in China as an anesthetic during surgery. There are several explanations for its effectiveness: some contend it creates the placebo effect; others, as already noted, that it stimulates the production of natural opioids (see Han 2004), which itself is sometimes taken to be the general functioning of the placebo effect; recently it has been suggested that acupuncture stimulates the wound-healing qualities of fibroblast cells in "connective tissue proper" of the body (Langevin 2013); and others suggest that it stimulates the closure of spinal "gates" in relation to the Gate Control Theory discussed in Chapter 2. In fact, Patrick Wall, co-author of the Gate Control Theory (with Ronald Melzack), was invited to witness surgery undergone with acupuncture as the anesthetic and noticed that a patient's surgery had begun *before* acupuncture needles were inserted. Wall suggests that this event (along with another surgery he witnessed) demonstrated to him the great similarity of acupuncture to hypnosis insofar as the *suggestion* of painlessness—by the physicians, the theology (of the vital life force *ch'i* by which acupuncture has been traditionally explained), the tradition of its use, the focus in the operating theater—created the *effect* of painlessness (1999: 88–89). In any case, surgical anesthesia is a powerful example, and many studies of acupuncture demonstrate its effectiveness in stimulating pain relief.

Studies have shown that hypnosis is more effective in pain relief than acupuncture, psychotherapy, biofeedback, drug placebos, and even more effective than morphine, aspirin, or valium (Hardcastle 1999: 180; among others she cites Melzack and Perry 1975, Spinhoven 1988, Smith, Barabasz, and Barabasz 1996). In fact, evidence from PET scans suggests that hypnotism seems to create some of the effects of lobotomy (Hardcastle 1999: 117). Hypnosis is the inducement of the creation of a trance in a person, where ordinary functions of consciousness are lost and the subject is susceptible to increased responsiveness to suggestion. Patrick Wall argues that "the essence of the hypnotic state is only that the subject has agreed to hand over to the hypnotist the responsibility for deciding how they will react and what they will sense," and he goes on to note that "this is a common condition of everyday life," simply the acceptance of authority that can be seen in lawyers cross-examining witnesses, parents telling bedtime stories, and other such phenomena (1999: 86–87). In the late eighteenth century, the Austrian physician Franz Anton Mesmer created what he called "animal magnetism" as a treatment of healing diseases and suspending pain during surgery by means of hypnosis. Mesmer's theory was repudiated by commissions established by the King of France (one of which was headed by Benjamin Franklin), but in the late nineteenth century another physician, James Braid, studied the phenomenon and coined the term *hypnosis*, derived from the name of the Greek god of sleep, Hypnos. As early as 1826, hypnosis was used as an anesthetic in surgery (Hardcastle 1999: 182).

Today there remains some debate about how hypnosis, as both analgesia and anesthesia, creates its effects. On the one hand, there is some evidence that hypnosis modulates the perception but not the sensation of pain. In 1836 B. H. West noted that during a molar extraction a hypnotized patient had "a flush over the whole face and a slight quivering of the lip, with a countenance indicative of considerable pain" (1836: 351), and Hardcastle notes at some length that involuntary autonomic responses to pain occur during hypnosis (see Hardcastle 1999: 186–89). David Morris quotes the novelist, Reynolds Price, who suffered from excruciating chronic pain as the result of successful treatment of spinal cancer—an instance of neuropathic pain caused by damage to the central nervous system—describing the effects of hypnosis on his pain: "I'd grown essentially free from pain. Not free from its constant presence in my body—it roars on still, round the clock every day, in my back and legs and across my shoulders—but free from any real notice of it or concern for its presence" (1998: 116). (One treatment for pain often discussed is the simple *distraction* from it, finding ways for those in pain to think of something else. See, for instance, Brand and Yancey 1997: 253–56; and Thernstrom 2010: 297ff. Thernstrom notes that "hypnosis is an extreme form of controlling attention by which the brain is able to exclude from consciousness all unwanted external stimuli, including pain" [2010: 297].) On the other hand, there is also good evidence that hypnosis alters physiological responses to pain: it can reduce the number as well as the pain of migraines; it can change gastric acidic secretions in patients with irritable bowel syndrome; it can decrease inflammation with burns (Hardcastle 1999: 189); and there are documented cases of hypnosis eliminating warts (Ramachandran and Blakeslee 1998: 218). In other words, hypnosis—like acupuncture, like the placebo effect, like pain itself—suggests that the strict division between physiology and psychology does not allow us to fully understand the degree to which facts/events and experiences/perceptions interact in human life.

Palliative Care

Palliative care is the treatment of terminally ill people aiming at the improvement of the quality of life by means of the prevention and treatment of pain and suffering. The founding of the palliative care movement is usually attributed to Dame Cicely Saunders, who opened the St. Christopher's Hospice in London in 1967, although it was not accepted as a medical discipline in the United States until 2006. Such care is given in hospitals, homes, and special facilities, and it is organized around patient need rather than biomedical diagnosis. Dr. Eric Cassell articulates three goals of palliative care aimed at reducing pain and suffering to patients and their families:

- focus on the patient, not the disease;
- maximize the patient's function, not length of life;
- minimize pain and suffering to both the patient and her family. (1991: 241)

In many ways, the hospice care of palliative medicine treats the starkest instances of human pain. As Dr. Therese Vanier of St. Christopher's Hospice explained to Paul Brand:

> Pain from a terminal disease is unique. Pain from a bone fracture, sore tooth, childbirth, or even postoperative recovery has meaning, and there is an end in sight. Pain from progressive cancer has no meaning except the constant reminder of approaching death. For many of the patients who come to us, pain fills the entire horizon. They can't eat, sleep, pray, think, or relate to people without being dominated by pain. Here at St. Christopher's we try to combat that particular kind of pain.
>
> (Brand and Yancey 1997: 256–57)

Among other methods Saunders developed at St. Christopher's was patient self-medication (she found patients rarely over-medicated themselves), accommodations that allowed patients to be with other patients (not isolated in their illness) and that had room for overnight stays for family members, gardens and parks outside windows, concerts, and off-campus excursions. "St. Christopher's," Brand notes, has "incorporated nearly everything I have learned about pain management": hospice workers "allow for diversion and conscious distraction. They help soothe the subjective factors (fear, anxiety) that contribute to pain. They work hard to make the patient feel like a partner, not a victim, one who retains control over his or her own body. They create a caring community" (Brand and Yancey 1997: 258).

This chapter has surveyed areas and specifics of the treatment of pain with the aim, in large part, to demonstrate that the strategies of care also help us understand the nature of pain altogether, its combination of physiological–sensory events and psychological–perceptual experiences. The range of treatments examined here—from surgery to hospice care—demonstrates this constant combination, even as the emphasis of focus changes from the physiological facts of pain to its perceptual experience.

PART II
EXPERIENCES OF PAIN

5

THE EXPERIENCE OF PAIN: THE NATURE OF SUFFERING AND THE MEANING OF PAIN

Every one of us will know pain in our lives, and none of us knows when it will come or how long it will stay. Although we will one day have effective treatment for the disease of chronic pain, we can never eradicate pain itself, because our bodies require it. Pain is a defining aspect of mortal life, a hallmark of what it means to be human. It often stamps both the beginning and the end of life. It threatens our deepest sense of ourselves and—portending death—reminds us of the ultimate disappearance of that self. It is the most vivid experience we can never quite describe, returning us to the wordless misery of infancy. It seems to rend a hole in ordinary reality; it is intrinsic to the human body, yet feels alien. And it is the aspect of mortality that we like least; we abhor pain more, even, than death.

—Melanie Thernstrom, *The Pain Chronicles*
(2010: 12)

Chapter 4 examined various treatments of pain both to describe responses to its ubiquitous experience and also to help clarify, in examining treatments of pain, the nature of pain itself as both a fact and an experience. Still, Part I takes as its starting point the examination of the

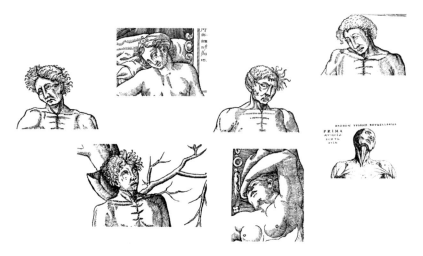

Figure 5.1 The Experience of Pain

fact/event of pain from the point of view of physiology and neurology, even if such an examination necessarily entails the experience/perception of pain as well insofar as pain is an *irreducibly complex* phenomenon. This chapter—and indeed, the whole of Part II—take as a starting point the experience of pain. To this end, this chapter examines differences in the *quality* of pain across cultures and across different moments in a lifetime, and especially the difference in quality of chronic as opposed to acute pain; it examines the nature of suffering in relation to these qualitative differences; and finally it examines what Dr. Paul Brand calls "intensifiers of pain" (Dr. Scott Fishman calls them "pain magnifiers" (2012: 9)). These intensifiers cut across all instances of pain—and particularly chronic pain—and affect particular aspects of the ways that pain is experienced. But more than this, they suggest, from the point of view of experience rather than the point of view of physiology, ways that sufferers and their caretakers can engage and deal with pain to the end of mitigating its effects on lived life.

An Element of Blank

In order to focus on the experience of pain itself, this chapter begins by examining the representations of pain as it is expressed in a poem and narrated in a memoir, representations returned to throughout this chapter. The generalized representation of the experience of pain as such in Emily Dickinson's poem and in Lous Heshusius's vivid description of her experience of neuropathic pain in *Inside Chronic Pain* (already mentioned in Chapter 1) allows us to encounter a sense of the harrowing *absolute* experience of both acute and chronic pain. Here is Dickinson's short poem, written in the late nineteenth century:

Pain—has an Element of Blank —
It cannot recollect
When it begun—or if there were
A time when it was not —

It has no Future—but itself —
Its Infinite realms contain
Its Past—enlightened to perceive
New Periods—of Pain.

(poem 650; 2004)

In this poem, pain becomes not a condition but a thing, an agent in the world that could, but does not remember; that could, but does not have expectations outside itself; that feels itself to be "Infinite" and, indeed, *absolute*. (Later in this chapter [pp. 89–90] Elaine Scarry's harrowing description of the *absoluteness* of pain offers a fine paraphrase and commentary on this poem.) The *agency* of pain in Dickinson's poem— Dr. David Biro describes "the language of agency" as one of three recurrent metaphors in patient descriptions of pain (2010: 16)—is very different from the *non-agency* of pain described in Chapter 6 in relation to experiences of pain in connection to religious experience. Under the category of agency, as we saw in Lous Heshusius's account of chronic pain in Chapter 1, pain *actively* "obliterates the past, torments the present, and makes the future unbearable before the fact" (2009: 25). This experience constitutes the "Element of Blank" Dickinson describes.

Reading Dickinson's poem in relation to her own experience of chronic pain, Melanie Thernstrom struggles between understanding the experience of pain as an active source of suffering and understanding pain as a simple "non-active" physiological condition:

You try to wake yourself out of pain—*it's not an infinite realm,
it's a neurological disease*—but you can't. You are in a dreamscape
that is familiar yet horribly altered, one in which you are
yourself—but not. You want to return to your real self—life and
body—but the dream goes on and on. You tell yourself it's only
a nightmare—a product of not-yet-fully understood brain
chemistry. But to be in pain is to be unable to awaken: the veil
of pain through which you cannot see, the vale of pain in which
you have lost your way.

(2010: 17)

Although Thernstrom takes up the vocabulary of western religion in her
pun on veil/vale to articulate both the sensation and the perception of
pain, the desire to return to her "real" life and body is very different
from the desire, found in certain religious experiences (as we shall see)
to abandon "self" to different kinds of transcendence in relation to the
experience of pain.

We are not clear about the sources of Dickinson's pain—she herself
suffered from a prolonged and painful condition of her eye, and throughout her life she endured experiences of fearfulness, loneliness, and isolation in relation to pain, experiences explicitly discussed at the end of this
chapter—but it is clear that Heshusius, like Thernstrom, suffers from
neuropathic pain after a terrible automobile accident. Earlier chapters
touched upon some possible interrelated causes of neuropathic pain where
pain does not function adaptively as an alarm for imminent damage, actual
damage, and the healing of damage, but instead becomes a *disease* in its
own right: damage to the central nervous system (as in Alphonse Daudet
and Reynolds Price), the sensitization of the central nervous system,
reorganization of neural pathways, pathological triggering of pain
schemas. Heshusius narrates the story of her pain, "approximately 8,700
hours of severe pain, 7,200 hours of considerable pain, and 11,500 hours
of light pain. In all, 27,000 hours of pain over an eleven-year period. This
means an average of approximately seven hours of pain each day, every
day" (2009: 7). Moreover, she notes that "the most pervasive problem of
the chronic pain experience, apart from the torment of the pain itself, is
its inexpressibility and its invisibility" (2009: 14). Thus, when friends

learned that she was not terminally ill, they thought she was normal, that she "just" had pain: "'You're strong, you'll get over this,' a friend told me cheerfully and with great conviction. That was in 1998. 'I just know you will beat this. I feel it,' said another friend in 2002" (2009: 18). Moreover, she notes, "one does *not* become inured to constant pain. On the contrary. Pain is always new. Over time the neurological system, being continually aroused, can become so hyperreactive that the slightest thing can trigger the pain mode" (2009: 19). One feature of pain recurrently described in narrative descriptions of pain is the fact that although pain is "always new" to those who suffer it, it easily becomes "old" and easily dismissed by those encountering its report.

For Heshusius, as for Dickinson, pain encompasses "Infinite realms [that] contain/Its Past":

> I would look at pictures of myself taken in the years before the accident and have a hard time remembering 'her' as myself. The pictures show a young and energetic-looking woman. I had done all these things I was doing in the photo. Been to all those places. But by the time the pain was at its worst, I had become someone else. 'A crumbled woman,' is how one of my daughters described me.
>
> (2009: 26)

Indeed, when she meets one of the few sympathetic physicians she goes to—one of the "fine ones" she describes in her memoir—and tells him about "the long, severe Toronto winters that made the pain worse and the isolation unbearable" and that also created a situation where she had to move "four times in five years," he tells her: "You have lost a life"; and she thinks, "finally, someone who got it" (2009: 61).

As this suggests, for Heshusius another constantly frustrating—and indeed *painful*—aspect of her illness was her encounters with doctors, and much of her striking account of living with chronic pain illness focuses on her relationships with physicians and other healthcare workers. In fact, she notes that "since for many of us chronic pain remains resistant to treatment, the patient-doctor relationship is both crucial and demanding" (2009: 76). She had seen twenty-two doctors and specialists and many alternative healthcare workers as a consequence of her accident. (In her lifetime, Dickinson had seen a train of physicians as well.) "There have been the gentle ones," Heshusius notes:

> The rude ones. The attentive ones. The nonlistening ones. The truly caring ones. The clearly uncaring ones. The humble ones. The arrogant ones. The broadly informed ones. The narrowly trained ones. The ones who have no time for you. The ones who try to have time for you.
>
> (2009: 45)

She watches their eyes, their body language, their choice of words, their gestures to figure out whether or not they "get it," and most of the time they don't. But the "fine ones" do, and what they do is instructive: they spend time talking, they build trust by being open about lack of knowledge, they perform careful hands-on examinations, touching and feeling (as opposed to only reading tests and reports), they ask her about her sleep, they are "friendly yet to-the-point," they never display impatience (2009: 60–64), and they never give the impression that they are working for pharmaceutical companies. (Among other things, Heshusius notes that what are called "side effects [of pain drugs] . . . are effects that alter life in major ways," that "a principal source of disorder and disease *is* disconnection, meaning the inability to attend to relevant feedback from the body" which is an *effect* of many pain medications [2009: 89].) In *engaging* with chronic pain—acknowledging its existence, its costs in pain, relationships, and the very *kinds* of suffering in the various categories that create and condition suffering examined later in this chapter—the "fine" healthcare workers return some measure of humanity to the blank of pain both Heshusius and Dickinson describe. The simple act of acknowledging pain on the part of caretakers—"I see you are in terrible pain; I am sorry that this is so"—goes a long way toward erasing the blank of pain.

Sensitivity to Pain

Although this chapter focuses on experiences of pain, it is important to note empirical evidence and systematic measurements that have been developed to describe pain sensitivity in relation to physiology as well as perception/experience. Sensitivity to pain is measured in three ways. The first way measures, on a cellular level, specific limit points at which various stimuli—i.e., thermal (burning or freezing), mechanical (pinching or pulling), or chemical (acids or poisons)—trigger nociceptor nerves to signal cell damage. (Heshusius experiences all these things.) These trigger points are common to all members of a species—they seem hardwired by evolution—and are only altered by disease processes, such as leprosy and diabetes, that destroy peripheral nerves. (Dr. Paul Brand's focus on pain began with his work with leprosy patients, and a significant portion of amputations associated with leprosy and diabetes is related to unfelt tissue damage caused by these diseases.) A second measure of pain sensitivity is called the *pain threshold*, the point at which the subject of pain perceives a stimulus to be painful. The pain threshold is a function of conscious perception, such as the point at which a sensation of warmth turns to the sensation of burning. Although it is not as uniform across a species as are the nociceptive triggers, the pain threshold is also fairly similar from individual to individual within a species. The third measure of pain sensitivity is called *pain tolerance*, and it measures what a person can endure. In experiments, for example, pain tolerance is the point at which a subject declares a painful stimulus unbearable and asks for it to be discontinued. (For a fuller account of sensitivity measures see Thernstrom 2010: 174; her description is followed here). Pain tolerance depends not only on the temperament of the individual but also on the circumstances of the pain and thus can vary dramatically not only between people with different personal and cultural backgrounds, but in a particular person in different situations. Fishman notes that a person can hold her hand in a bowl of ice and water and measure the time it takes for the sensation to feel painful: this is the pain threshold. She can continue to hold her hand in the ice water and measure the time before she has to remove it: this is pain tolerance. One person might hold her hand in the water to the point of frostbite while another redraws her hand at the first flash of pain (2000: 19–21). Those suffering chronic pain have no choice: they live, so to speak, at the point of frostbite.

Schemas of Experience, Schemas of Pain

The experience of pain, measured in these ways, has led Melanie Thernstrom to describe the complexity of pain experience altogether. "Is pain sensation, emotion, or idea?," she asks.

> Is it a product of biology or culture? If it is primarily a biological phenomenon, then why does it seem to vary so much from person to person and from culture to culture? If it is primarily a cultural one, then why does it seem so universal? After all, there is a word for headache in every language, ancient and modern. When the ancient Babylonian describes the headache that envelops like a garment, we know exactly what he means.
>
> (2010: 281)

With these questions, she is noting the complex actuality that pain is both a fact and an experience where one or the other description cannot be taken as primary. As an event, it lends itself to the precise measurements of the "law-like" (nomological) and even descriptive sciences; as an experience it lends itself to the accountings of the schemas of experience and action. (For a discussion of these terms, see Appendix I.)

Although the nature of cognitive and experiential schemas was described in Chapter 3, because the creation of patterns of attention and expectation that schemas condition is so important to the *quality* of our responses to and engagements with pain—and, indeed, with experiences in and interactions with the world more generally—it is necessary to examine schema theory more fully in the context of focusing on the experience of pain in relation to biology and culture. "A schema (or frame, as it is sometimes called)" is:

> a pattern of concepts, meanings, and associations produced from memory traces, present experiences, and expectations of the future. Our schemata are ever changing and constantly updating, reflecting the ongoing stream of perception and thought in our mental lives. David Rumelhart describes them as follows: '[S]chemata emerge at the moment they are needed from the

interaction of large numbers of much simpler elements, all working in concert with one another . . . [Schemata] are not explicit entities, but rather are implicit in our knowledge and are created by the very environment that they are trying to interpret as it is interpreting them" [Rumelhart et al. 1986] . . . [S]imple sensory stimuli can trigger a full-blown meaningful schema . . . [and] there is no reason why pain, one sort of sensory stimulus, cannot do this, nor why we cannot have schemata for pain that other things might trigger.

(Hardcastle 1999: 119)

As this suggests, such schemas are *provisional* because even while the event and experience of pain sensory inputs are assimilated into pre-existing schemas, the event/experience of that assimilation itself in turn can modify the schema (Hardcastle 1995: 79; she cites Mandler 1984, Minsky 1981, 1986, Rumelhart 1980, Schank and Abelson 1977). See Exhibit 5.1. In fact, schema theory accounts for both the universal and idiosyncratic nature of the experience of pain Thernstrom describes insofar as pain as an experience is a function of *attention and expectation* even while as a fact/event it is also a function of the regularity of its affect. (Hardcastle is repeatedly cited throughout this section because

---

EXHIBIT 5.1

Dr. Jerry Vannatta and I note in *The Chief Concern of Medicine* that "the acceptance of a particular schema is always *provisional* in that further evidence can lead to its abandonment or revision. Thus our felt sense that a room *is* a classroom as we apprehend salient features, such as a blackboard, bookshelves, chairs—the apprehension of features that conditions our *experience* as well as our understanding as we enter that room—can be understood, upon encountering further evidence, that it is a stage set or a nursery" (2013: 15–16). Robert Ornstein describes the manner in which right hemisphere brain damage reduces—and sometimes erases—the possibility of revising initial schemas (1997: 109; see also Schleifer 2009: 142–45). Among other things, the *provisional* nature of schemas underlines their *active* functioning (rather than simply being passive, automatic responses as in Pavlovian "conditioning").

she offers extensive surveys of work in cognitive psychology, neuro-physiology, and clinical neurology that are useful in focusing on the experience of pain without losing sight of understanding pain as a fact/event as well.)

In any case, schemas of experience, as many cognitive scientists and neurologists argue, categorize and condition the *quality* of sensory experience so that what appears as *immediate* sensory consciousness is already the result of an initial level of processing that has taken place "prior to any conscious experience" (Steen 2005: 93; in this analysis he cites Edelman 1992). This is perhaps more easily grasped when we think of how different patterns of sound—another sensory system—create the feeling of the "naturalness" of music in one's own culture and the strange, almost "non-musical" sounds from a foreign culture. Such categorization and conditioning are organized in terms of schemas of experience and understanding, which are both inherited and learned (and hence universal and idiosyncratic). Moreover, insofar as they are learned (i.e., "acquired"), the *quality* of experience—which is to say, of consciousness itself—is intimately connected with memory. This, in part, is why the amnesic agents described in Chapter 1 retrospectively rendered the experience of pain of Dr. Vertosick's patient non-existent. (The connection between pain and memory is also why, as we shall see later in Chapter 6, physicians and others for a long time assumed that infants do not "feel" pain.)

As mentioned in Chapter 2, psychologists and neurologists describe two kinds of memory systems, the second of which is closely linked to the acquired schemas of experience. The first memory system is procedural memory, which describes skills and habits. Many psychologists call this "implicit memory" rather than procedural memory because not all such memories result in action responses (such as unconscious muscular actions that balance a bicycle rider); that is, many of the learned human habitual responses to stimuli (such as the immediate, context-free memory of a word's meaning upon hearing it) do not involve (motor) action as such (Hardcastle 1995: 80). Implicit memory is *automatic* and *unconscious*: we do not consciously remember that "tree" is a sound that designates that woody object, but seemingly automatically and seemingly immediately grasp that meaning. The second memory system describes explicit (or, "episodic") memory. Explicit memory is controlled, context-

rich, and creates the *experience* of consciousness by means of accessing—
and sometimes modifying—learned and inherited schemas of experience
(Hardcastle 1995: 155). (For the experimental basis of the distinction
between these two memory systems, see Derruchat and Baveux 1989,
Gordon 1988, Mandler 1984, Schacter 1985, Schacter and Moscovitch
1984, Squire 1987, whom Hardcastle cites 1995: 200. Donald also
provides detailed descriptions of experiments that demonstrate this
distinction 1991: 150–51.) The explicit memory system, some argue,
"forms the basis for short-term memory and consciousness itself"
(Hardcastle 1995: 81), including the conscious experience of pain. "Our
pain system" gives rise to "sorts of organized behavior" so that "pain [as]
one sort of sensory stimulus" can "trigger a full-blown meaningful
schema." Moreover, "once the pain schema is activated"—as we have
seen in Dickinson, Thernstrom, and Heshusius—"it becomes impossible
not to pay attention to it" (Hardcastle 1999: 89, 119).

Elaine Scarry makes this same argument that "pain begins by being
'not oneself' and ends by having eliminated all that is 'not itself.'" She
goes on:

> At first occurring only as an appalling but limited internal fact,
> it eventually occupies the entire body and spills out into the
> realm beyond the body, takes over all that is inside and outside,
> makes the two obscenely indistinguishable, and systematically
> destroys anything like language or world extension that is
> alien to itself and threatening to its claims. Terrifying for its
> narrowness, it nevertheless exhausts and displaces all else until
> it seems to become the single broad and omnipresent fact of
> existence.
>
> (1985: 54–55)

In this passage Scarry offers a fine analysis of the *experience* of pain that
Dickinson's poem enacts and represents (see also pp. 113–16 below).
The narrow intensity of pain she describes is a physiological *fact*, but it
also seems almost *pure attention* that triggers, and perhaps exacerbates,
self-fulfilling *expectations*. It is as if pain experience reduces schemas to
almost absolute narrowness: after all "language or world extension" are

each closely tied to schemas of experience. In this, attention and expectation—like implicit and explicit memory—seem to become identical, almost "obscenely indistinguishable": surely this is what Dickinson means when she says that pain "has no Future—but itself" and can perceive nothing but "New Periods—of Pain."

In any case, these two "memory systems," which might collapse into one another in the complex fact and experience of pain, together:

> process incoming stimuli as well as store previous experiences because there is actually little distinction between the storage of previous perceptions and processing current ones. In particular, mental states use the information stored ... to 'interpret' incoming data such that they fit into meaningful units or schemas.
>
> (Hardcastle 1995: 95)

Thus, the processing giving rise to the conscious experience of pain takes place by means of schemas of experience in such a way that "memory and perception are inextricably bound together" (Hardcastle 1995: 81–82, 84; compare this to Kandel's physiological description of the memory of pain discussed in Chapter 2). This processing giving rise to seeming "immediate" experience—based upon wide citations of empirical studies in cognitive psychology, neurophysiology, and clinical neurology (Hardcastle 1995: 71)—suggests that (1) the measures of pain sensitivity founded on the *automatic* inherited species-functioning of nociceptive nerves, (2) the *perceptive* functioning of the pain threshold, at which point warmth is perceived as burning, and (3) the *controlled* functioning of pain tolerance can all be understood in relation to the two kinds of memory that cognitive science and neuroscience describe and that Dickinson suggests in her poem: like implicit memory, pain in the poem "cannot recollect/When it begun—or if there were/A time when it was not"; yet at the same time, like explicit memory, it is "enlightened to perceive/New Periods—of Pain." These two modalities of memory are closely connected to the attention and expectation generated by schemas of experience.

EXHIBIT 5.2

Besides schemas conditioning experience derived from life-experience and from "vicarious" experiences that families and cultures provide us to develop attention and expectations, other schemas are inherited from the deep time of species adaptation. This is most clear, I think, in the schemas of languages acquisition that share, as Noam Chomsky and others have argued, a kind of universal grammar. While different languages are not intelligible to those "outside" them, the *propensity* to acquire language schemas is a universal human trait (like the propensity to walk). Persuasive arguments have been made for a similarly inherited propensity to develop neurological schemas for the experiences of narrative cognition, of the various cultural forms of music, and, as we have seen in Hardcastle and the scientists she cites, of pain experiences (see Schleifer and Vannatta 2013; Steen 2005; Mithen 2006; Hardcastle 1995, 1999). The concept and phenomenon of "propensity" erases the stark opposition between nature and nurture, physiological "fact" and human "experience."

Cross-Cultural Pain

In this context, the measures of pain tolerance and, perhaps to a lesser extent, the pain threshold describe measurable differences in the *quality* of pain experience, and such quality, as evidence from cognitive and neuroscience suggests, is determined to large extent by means of the *schemas* one acquires from one's environment—from previous stimuli (personal explicit memories), family, and culture (social explicit memories)—all of which establish the schemas that shape and condition experience itself (see Exhibit 5.2). The provisional nature of experiential schemas is closely connected to action in particular situations: thus, a severely injured person can painlessly walk away from an automobile accident. As we have seen, Hardcastle suggests that this behavior is the result of a neurological Pain Inhibitory System, but even if her specific speculations are not correct, there is good evidence that some kind of neurological pain-modulatory system does exist: thus there is experimental evidence that "electrical stimulation of parts of the brain involved in the pain-modulatory system (the periaqueductal gray matter and raphe magnus nucleus) produces not simply some pain relief, but *complete* analgesia in both humans and animals" (Thernstrom 2010: 290). This pain-modulatory system is "activated by various cognitive and affective states, the two most important of which are *attention* and *expectation*" (Thernstrom 2010: 290), which is to say it is activated by certain *kinds* of experience conditioned by schemas acquired as cultural norms.

In his work on the relationship between culture and pain—both *The Culture of Pain* and *Illness and Culture in the Postmodern Age*—David Morris consistently argues that neither illness more generally nor pain more specifically is "a purely biological state . . . but rather something in part created or interpenetrated by culture" (1998: 70–71). By "culture" he means "common sense," or, in other words, the particular horizons of *possible experiences* that are conditioned and delineated by shared meanings and understandings, which are often not fully consciously grasped. (Exhibit 3.1 offers the specific example of how particular languages determine what qualities of sound—such as the tonal pitch of a sound—demand attention and expectation. Such attention and expectation delimit what is usually *experienced* [i.e., "the horizons of *possible experiences*"] in a particular culture.) The particular experience Morris focuses on is pain. In the framework presented here, the horizons of experience—both the meaning and the "feel" of such experience—are conditioned by schemas that organize *attention and expectation*, which are shared by a group of people living together in a certain time and place. Morris focuses on time: what he describes, by and large, is the trans-formations in the meaning and experience of pain over time, from biblical times when Job questions the pain he encounters to contemporary times when pain occasions "the impulse to phone our local physician, which seems now almost instinctive and certainly belongs to the domain of absolute common sense" (1991: 34). That is, focusing on felt experiences, he examines "the particular changeable nature of pain—its power to take on new meaning or abruptly to lose, to regain, or to transform the meaning it temporarily possesses." Such an understanding, he argues, "requires that we understand this most ancient and personal of human experiences as indelibly stamped by a specific place and time" (1991: 37).

Although Morris emphasizes *meaning* in this description, it is more important to be mindful that cultural formations transform the very *experience* of pain. Thus, in one example Morris sets forth, he notes how:

pain, as a lived experience, may come to *include* the culturally created and reinforced meaning that a person is dysfunctional. In Lithuania, for example, where drivers do not carry personal-injury insurance, rear-end automobile collisions fail to produce the lingering headaches and intractable neck pains notorious in Western democracies, where insured motorists receive compensation for chronic whiplash or whiplash syndrome. Norway, by contrast, [a country in the same part of Europe] with a total population of 4.2 million, has 70,000 people in a patients' organization claiming chronic disability from whiplash injuries.

(1998: 122–23)

Morris is focusing on the *individual* experience of pain, but in a *social* example presented in Chapter 6, the anthropologist Valentine Daniel describes a collective experience of pain in relation to the religious experiences of people participating in the forty-mile Hindu (Ayyappan) barefoot pilgrimage for several days over blisteringly hot stony roads. This painful experience, as we shall see, participates in the social transformation of the meaning and experience of pain—its *perception*—just as Morris describes the transformation of the experience and meaning of whiplash. (In *The Spirit Catches You and You Fall Down* Anne Fadiman similarly contrasts the experience of pain in birthing in western cultures and southeast Asian Hmong culture [1998: 3–11].) This should be made distinctly clear: Morris is not arguing about embroidery, exaggeration, dissimulation, self-delusion. He is arguing (and Daniel and Fadiman demonstrate) that *pain* itself—the fact and experience of pain—is conditioned by acquired schemas, cultural norms, that make the conscious experience of pain what it is.

The phenomenon of conditioned experience has been demonstrated in non-human animals as well. Ronald Melzack, whose work in pain studies has been noted throughout this book, began his scholarly work in psychology by raising Scottish terrier pups in padded cages where they did not encounter any of the ordinary bruises or hurt of growing up. He discovered that, with this upbringing, they did not manifest basic responses to pain. They did not react when their paws were pricked, and when they encountered a flaming match they poked their noses into it and sniffed, and even when their flesh burned, they showed no signs of pain or distress (Brand and Yancey 1997: 206; Jackson 2002: 332–33; it should be added that such experiments systematically inflicting pain on animals—and particularly our close relatives, apes—are not as acceptable as they were when Melzack worked in the 1950s). Melzack's experiment suggested that much of what is called pain is learned—or, as I prefer to say, "actively conditioned"—and is not simply an immediate sensation. Paul Brand adds that "whether consciously or subconsciously, the mind largely determines how we perceive pain. Laboratory tests reveal that, like Melzack's terriers, people reared in different cultural environments experience pain differently" (Brand and Yancey 1997: 208). Marni Jackson notes that cultural norms in relation to the treatment of children—something returned to in Chapter 6—also affect the "horizon" of possible pain experience: "early suffering," she writes, describing implicit rather than explicit memory, "sets our thermostat for how we respond to later insults and injuries. For some, affliction becomes a kind of default setting. Neglect opens up channels for pain that may never close. In this way, pain trains us. All sorts of cultural conditions—child-rearing customs that teach us to ignore a crying baby—may end up contributing to chronic pain conditions later in life" (2002: 134). She is describing acquired patterns of attention and expectation—acquired schemas of experience—conditioned by *implicit memory* that determines in part the particular quality or "feel" of pain.

As we have already seen, the functions of attention and expectation make the quality of chronic pain very different from that of acute pain. By definition, acute pain ends: and by ending, it takes on the felt-meaning of doing the positive work of pain described in Chapter 2, the work of alarm, protection, preventing further harm, healing. This is captured in the sports slogan, "No pain, no gain." But the *quality* of chronic pain is different: there is no—or little—"positive" outcome from pain that seems to do no work other than to create suffering. Many of the books cited throughout this study—Lous Heshusius's *Inside Chronic Pain: An Intimate and Critical Account*, Melanie Thernstrom's *The Pain Chronicles*, Alphonse Daudet's *In the Land of Pain*, Brand and Yancey's *The Gift of Pain*, Frank Vertosick's *Why We Hurt*, Scott Fishman's *The War on Pain* and *Listening to Pain*—repeatedly recount experiences of futility, isolation, anger, sorrow, bereavement, futurelessness, the very *blank* of pain Dickinson describes, as the narrow quality of lived-life people face who live lives of chronic pain. In the case of chronic pain, *attention* is reduced to and sharply focused on the overwhelming felt-sense of pain that offers little room for attention to anything else; and *expectation* is simply and narrowly focused on more of the same as other forms of remembered and expected life fade from memory. (While torture, which is a major focus of Scarry's study, is a form of acute pain, it shares with chronic pain the lack of any positive "alarm" functions and the extreme narrowing of attention and expectation.)

The Nature of Suffering

This account of narrow horizons of attention and expectation that pain creates makes explicit what is implicit throughout this book: that pain and suffering are closely tied together, particularly in the experience of chronic pain. In a powerfully insightful book, *The Nature of Suffering and the Goals of Medicine*, Dr. Eric Cassell gives a simple but profound definition of suffering. He defines suffering as "the state of severe distress associated with events that threaten the intactness of person" (1991: 33). The experience of pain is a significant (but not the sole) source of such a threat to personhood. Cassell notes that "people in pain frequently report suffering from pain when they feel out of control, when the pain is overwhelming, when the source of the pain is unknown, when the meaning of the pain is dire, or when the pain is apparently without end" (1991: 36). Thernstrom describes the connection between pain and suffering much more clinically, distinguishing between pain that threatens identity and "chosen pain"—in childbirth, tattoos, athletics, battle—that is "*integrative*" and strengthens the intactness of personhood. She notes that suffering is the result of "unchosen disintegrative pain: pain that cannot be reconciled with one's sense of self, but undermines and destroys it, as the pain of surgery differs from the pain of disease, even when they result in the same tissue damage" (2010: 201).

In his account of suffering, Cassell describes salient features of "personhood" that are threatened in the experience of pain, and particularly chronic pain. "Persons," he says:

> have personality and character, a lived past, a family, a family's lived past, culture and society, roles, associations with others, a

political dimension, activities, day-to-day behaviors, an existence below awareness, a body, a secret life, a believed-in future, and a transcendent dimension. The importance of these features for understanding suffering is that each can be affected by illness [and overwhelming pain] and become a source of suffering if the integrity of the person is thereby disrupted.

(1991: 160)

The Catholic mystic Simone Weil describes suffering—she uses the term "affliction" in her theological vocabulary—in terms that resonate with Cassell's even if they do not have his powerful specificity:

affliction is anonymous before all things; it deprives its victims of their personality and makes them into things. It is indifferent; and it is the coldness of this indifference—a metallic coldness— that freezes all those it touches right to the depths of their souls. They will never find warmth again. They will never believe any more that they are anyone.

(Weil 2001: 125)

Both Weil and Cassell put in mind images of both painful and painless suffering set forth in Chapter 1: Lous Heshusius's account of finding herself become a strange pain-ridden person whose pain "obliterates the past, torments the present, and makes the future unbearable before the fact" (2009: 25); and Paul Brand's description of the transformation of the leprous man's foot into an apparently inanimate object.

Cassell's analysis of suffering should not suggest that pain and suffering can be understood in terms of the opposition between physical and mental pain. Pain, as has been demonstrated throughout this book, is irreducibly complex: as Morris argues, "in perceiving our pain, we transform it from a simple sensation into the complex mental-emotional events that psychologists and philosophers call perception" (1991: 29; see also 1998: 118). Moreover, what is remarkable about the detailed characteristics of personhood threatened by pain that Cassell analyzes is that most, if not all, of them can be defined or described in terms of schemas of experience. That is, the *overwhelming* experience of pain overwhelms, precisely, the *order* of cognition and experience that schemas create by imposing relationship onto events (Mandler 1984: 51). It has already been suggested that pain narrows and collapses schemas, and as we will see in Chapter 6—it has also been touched upon here—Scarry offers a powerful analysis of torture that can be understood as the systematic destruction of experience grasped and lived as orderly in the ways that Cassell suggests that family, culture, bodily life, forms of ordinary and extraordinary *attention*, and, perhaps, above all, *expectations* of a lived future create the sense of an orderly lived life. (Dickinson's poem particularly emphasizes the sense of *futurelessness* that pain provokes.) That sense of orderly lived life and its component parts are destroyed by the fact that overwhelming pain reduces all time to the *blank moment* of pain itself: the narrowest attention and the destruction of expectation outside itself. Cassell says that suffering "has a temporal element" (1991: 36), but he means by this that the irresistible "immediate attack of physical pain" (Weil 2001) destroys the temporal nature of the elements of Cassell's catalogue, destroys the ordinary and comfortable experiences of lived life altogether.

Still, one function of human life that Cassell does not explicitly include in his catalogue is human speech itself, even if his categories of social and cultural life, roles, associations with others, depend strongly on language. Morris remarks that tragedy enacts suffering and, at its heights, as in *Oedipus*, sets forth a "cry of agony: speech rolled back into mere sound and torment": he notes that Lear, holding the corpse of his dead daughter, "utters three words, but they are not so much words as sounds, less spoken than bellowed like an animal cry: 'Howl, howl, howl.' As with Oedipus," he concludes, "we witness simply the ruined human body and the sound of suffering. Nothing more" (1991: 248). Pain and suffering destroy what I might call the "master" schema of personal and social experience, language itself: hence the futility, isolation, anger, sorrow, bereavement, futurelessness, and *blank* experience of pain we encountered earlier.

Intensifiers of Pain

As this should suggest, suffering intensifies the experience of pain. In a powerful chapter towards the end of the book, *The Gift of Pain*, Dr. Paul Brand catalogues a number of what calls "intensifiers of pain." The chapter begins with an authoritative indictment of institutional pain care:

If the hospice movement is designed to help patients face the final challenge of pain, the typical modern hospital seems designed to render its patients helpless before all pain. Confined to a private, sterile room, entangled in a web of tubes and wires, the object of knowing glances and whispered conversations, the patient feels trapped and alone. In this alien atmosphere, pain thrives. I sometimes wonder if pharmaceutical companies have masterminded the scheme of modern hospitals in an attempt to promote the use of pain-relieving medications.

(Brand and Yancey 1997: 261)

Brand explains that he uses the term "pain intensifiers" to describe responses of patients to their condition—especially in hospital rooms—that heighten the perception of pain for them. He lists five pain intensifiers: fear, anger, guilt, loneliness, and helplessness (1997: 262). Dr. Scott Fishman uses the term *pain magnifier* and also lists many of these aspects of pain experience in *Listening to Pain* (2012: 39).

Psychologists have isolated six primary emotions that display particular physiological and facial responses across all human cultures: fear (anxiety), anger, sadness (depression), disgust, joy, and surprise (startle-effect). In our 2013 book, *The Chief Concern of Medicine: The Integration of the Medical Humanities and Narrative Knowledge into Medical Practices*, Dr. Jerry Vannatta and I describe various "filters" that distort and confuse patient–physician interactions. Among these filters—besides age, class, gender, cultural background—we note that patients bring three of the six primary emotions—fear, anger, and sadness—to their encounters with physicians and, as Brand and Fishman suggest, to their encounters with pain as well. (The loneliness and helplessness that Brand mentions are instances of sadness; guilt combines all three emotions, and while Brand describes laboratory evidence to substantiate the ways fear and anger increase pain, he notes he "cannot point so precisely to a tangible root of guilt's effect on pain," although he adds that his long-term work with leprosy patients taught him that many patients feel "uniquely cursed by God" (Brand and Yancey 1997: 271)). Laboratory and hospital studies show that fear is the strongest intensifier of pain. The physiological responses to fear—such as muscle contraction that often pressures damaged nerves or creates spastic colon (unique to humans), heightened blood pressure, and reflex sympathetic dystrophy (RSD)—often exacerbate conditions giving rise to pain, and acquired schemas often create expectations that increase attention to and expectation of pain. (For example, parents can "teach" children to feel pain by suggesting that they are in pain when they fall. As we saw in Chapter 4, this is an instance of the element of "suggestiveness" found in hypnosis.) Similarly, anger gives rise to RSD, a condition that often occurs after "successful" surgery (of hands, joints, tendons) in which affected bodily areas experience increases in pain and painful stiffness. While infection might cause this condition, anger also provokes it. "Because of the sympathetic nervous system's close ties to the emotions," Brand concludes, a patient's anger in the face of a physician's lack of communication or outright disdain "can have a profound effect on the healing process" (Brand and Yancey 1997: 269). Brand even argues that in the United States litigious malpractice suits provide much ground "for anger, resentment, and frustration, the very feelings that foster conditions like reflect sympathetic dystrophy" (Brand and Yancey 1997: 270).

Brand doesn't examine sadness as such, but his discussions of the ways that loneliness and helplessness contribute to the experience of pain is profound. As already suggested, the experience of pain creates a strong asymmetrical difference between the *absolute* evidence of pain felt by the subject of pain and the almost equal strength of doubt felt by someone *outside* that experience: in *The Body in Pain*, Scarry notes that to have great pain is to have certainty; to hear that another person has pain is to have doubt (1985: 4). Speaking about her chronic pain in relation to her boyfriend, Kurt, Melanie Thernstrom notes that "always, I felt a little lonely in the relationship with Kurt, haunted by the sense that he didn't truly know me. Yet when I tried to think of what he didn't know about me, the only thing I could think of was pain" (2010: 78). Brand notes that such lonely sadness is exacerbated by modern hospital care. He describes how "in modern hospitals, patients often lie in solitude with nothing to focus on except their pain" and cites a study showing that private-room patients received an average of 13.4 doses of analgesic drugs while, in the same hospital, ward patients received 3.4 doses (Brand and Yancey 1997: 276). A final aspect of the loneliness of pain also emerges from the many narratives of pain I have read; a thorny but important aspect of the experience of pain to bring up, especially for healthcare workers. People in chronic pain are often simply difficult to be around. (Fishman devotes a chapter to this in *Listening to Pain* entitled "Dealing with Difficult Patients" [2012: ch. 4].) They are constantly distracted, self-centered, often angry, and can find ordinary interpersonal behaviors and gestures in those they interact with to be dismissive and hateful. Such behaviors (as Heshusius narrates in her memoir) can literally drive people away. Time and again as I read heart-wrenching accounts of people suffering from chronic pain, I saw often unconscious gestures of anger and blame directed at those around them. For health-care workers and other caretakers and companions, chronic pain requires deep patience and a constant sense that suffering is at the base of behavior and attitudes that necessitate that caring patience.

Finally, a sense of helplessness often accompanies pain, especially chronic pain. As we have already seen, Cassell notes that suffering in the face of pain in part is a function of the sense that the pain is "out of control," "overwhelming," and "apparently without end" (1991: 36). There are studies that confirm this: in laboratories, rats that can control a mild electric shock by manipulating a lever respond very differently from rats without such control, including the significant weakening of the latter's immune systems. Ronald Melzack says "It is also possible to change the level of pain by giving people the *feeling* that they have control over it even though, in fact, they do not. When burn patients are allowed to participate in the debridement of their burned tissues, they claim that the process is more bearable" (cited in Brand and Yancey 1997: 280). Chapter 7 in this book focuses on strategies to increase the sense of control—to decrease the sense of helplessness—in those who suffer pain.

All of these pain intensifiers are treatable. In our work, Dr. Vannatta and I have found the simple expedient of a physician explicitly bringing up the emotion she encounters in her patients with simple statements during patient–physician meetings—"You seem to be angry today"; "You seem frightened"; "You seem sad"—goes a long way toward dissipating or mitigating those emotions (2013: 196–200). Dr. Brand's experiences have led him to similar conclusions. "Together, doctor and patient," he notes, "we must face into the fear. What does the pain mean to the patient? Will the wage earner ever be able to support a family again? Will the hand ever look beautiful again? . . . I try to disarm fear by giving the patient honest, accurate information" (Brand and Yancey 1997: 264). Similarly, with anger, he tries to make explicit patients' source of anger— toward physicians? toward "fate"? toward the perceived human cause of pain (such as a drunk driver)?—in order to disarm the emotion as a contributing factor to pain. Loneliness as an intensifier of pain also can be addressed, with such institutional programs such as Brand describes in hospice care (see Chapter 4 above) and a wider sense of developing sites of community for people facing terrible pain. (This should be clear from the online references in Appendix II.) And he notes that "some chronic pain clinics battle helplessness by negotiating 'contracts' with their patients" by encouraging patients to articulate long-term goals such as "to play tennis, to walk a mile, to get a part-time job," and then, working together, staff and patients create smaller, weekly goals: "holding a tennis racket, walking across the room" (Brand and Yancey 1997: 281).

These strategies are instances of the larger strategy of healthcare Dr. Vannatta and I develop in *The Chief Concern of Medicine*: to make the explicit articulation of the patient's "chief concern"—what his condition, such as pain, means to him—so that together patient and physician can develop the agenda of care in relation to the patient's goals, desires, and needs. We created the notion of "chief concern" to be parallel to the first thing on the patient's official chart in the United States (the "History and Physical Exam"), the "chief complaint," and we hope that the protocols for the chart might explicitly include this category as something to be *part* of the official patient record physicians and others fill out. Discussion of the patient's concern will make discussions of fear, anger, and different forms of sadness explicit parts of healthcare and pain care to the end of mitigating the intensifiers of pain in those whose lives are filled with pain. It also makes it easier for caretakers simply to explicitly acknowledge the sufferer's pain, to say that they are sorry the sufferer encounters the fact/experience of pain. The final chapter of *Pain and Suffering*, "Caretakers and Sufferers Dealing with Pain," returns to this issue of the *actions* that knowledge of the experiences of pain and suffering calls for.

6

The Politics and Spirituality of Pain: Infants, Women, Torture, Religion, Pleasure and Pain

In the realm of suffering, affliction is something apart, specific, and irreducible. It is quite a different thing from simple suffering. It takes possession of the soul and marks it through and through with its own particular mark, the mark of slavery . . .

Affliction is an uprooting of life, a more or less attenuated equivalent of death, made irresistibly present to the soul by the attack of immediate apprehension of physical pain . . .

There is not real affliction unless the event that has seized and uprooted a life attacks it, directly or indirectly, in all its parts, social, psychological, and physical. The social factor is essential. There is not really affliction unless there is social degradation or the fear of it in some form or another.

—Simone Weil, "The Love of God and Affliction" (2001)

The French philosopher, Christian mystic, and political activist, Simone Weil, articulates explicitly what was strongly implicit in Chapter 5 (and, in fact, implicit throughout this book), namely that pain is always woven up with social as well as personal meaning. This is perhaps most implicit in Dr. Eric Cassell's delineation of the nature of suffering described

T Y P V s morborum & plagarum acciden=
tium ab extra corpori humano.

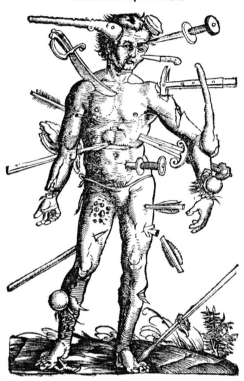

Figure 6.1 The Politics of Pain [Torture]

earlier, but it is also part of understandings of the phenomena of pain
as perception as well as sensation insofar as perception—like experience
—is tied up with schemas of apprehension, which are often cultural at
their source. This helps explain why Dr. Paul Brand emphasizes how
guilt is associated with pain; and it is notably implicit in the suggestion
of Elaine Scarry, when she contrasts the absolute destructiveness
of torture with human creativeness, that pain is involved with the "unmaking" and the "making" of the world itself. In other words, the
phenomena of human pain—its raw experience, its situation in personal
and social life, its creation of the necessity to make sense of its harrowing
facticity, and finally its uneasy relationship to its seeming opposite,

pleasure—all contribute to its place within the larger social contours in which we experience our lives. Because of this, pain lends itself to sociological as well as psychological study, and this chapter emphasizes the *social* as well as seemingly *personal* experience/perception of pain. In doing so, it unpacks an important implication in understanding pain experience in relation to schemas acquired from families and cultures described in Chapter 5.

Biases Related to Pain in Infants

The complexity of pain and its experience is most notable in the sometimes stark contrast between common-sense understandings of pain in relation to the fact/event of its physiology. That is particularly clear in the shocking recent history of social/medical attitudes towards infant pain. As we saw in Chapter 2, the IASP explicitly notes that "the inability to communicate verbally does not negate the possibility that an individual is experiencing pain and is in need of appropriate pain-relieving treatment" (IASP website), and as recently as 2002 (before this definition was posted) Marni Jackson noted that this addendum was being considered by the IASP "to avoid the possible suggestion that patients who can't articulate their pain—babies, or people with dementia, for instances—don't suffer pain" (2002: 21). The reason that many people thought otherwise—namely, that infants do not suffer pain—is closely linked to the implication of the amnesic drugs that Dr. Vertosick's heart patient took, the implication that pain is *necessarily* related to perception, which always requires memory, schemas, and the consciousness to which they give rise (see Exhibit 6.1). Thus, in her early study examining the nature of human consciousness, *Locating Consciousness*, Valerie Gray Hardcastle cites evidence that, like some hippocampal amnesiacs (amnesiacs who have lost short-term memory because of damage to the hippocampus, such as the phenomenon portrayed in the film *Momento*), infants cannot maintain short-term memory, but that infants, unlike hippocampal amnesiacs, do not even exhibit explicit, controlled memory ("semantic memory") (1995: 67–68, 214 n. 236); and she goes so far as to argue that "because infants cannot store incoming information in richly interconnected semantic networks—the only defining characteristic of conscious mnemonic processing that we have been able to uncover—we

---

EXHIBIT 6.1

In *The Myth of Pain*, Valerie Gray Hardcastle notes: "if you believe, as I have argued elsewhere, that . . . schemas are necessary for consciousness, then young infants cannot consciously experience pain, for they cannot consciously experience anything" (1999: 198).

---

should conclude that they are not conscious" (1995: 96; see Damasio 1999: 16–17 describing "extended consciousness"; and Edelman 2005: 8–9 describing "higher-order consciousness"). Since many, as noted throughout this book, assert that pain, by definition, must be conscious, it was concluded that infants, in a manner similar to Dr. Vertosick's patient, do not suffer a pain experience.

In her later study, *The Myth of Pain*, Hardcastle returns to the specific case of conscious pain in infants and modifies her earlier argument and maintains that "children experience pain differently from adults," citing studies that demonstrate that often children "feel more pain than adults do under similar circumstances." Nevertheless, she also describes the sociological fact of the consistent lack of treatment of pain for infants and children: writing in 1999, she notes that in the United States rarely (less than 30 percent of the time) do children undergoing bone marrow aspiration receive premedication; that in the 1970s and '80s less than 50 percent of children, aged four to eight, received any analgesia after surgery at hospitals; and that after undergoing surgery children were given paralytic drugs but not anesthesia in intensive care; and Melanie Thernstrom notes, astonishingly, that "until the late 1970s (this is not a typo), most surgeries in the United States and around the world were performed on infants with little or inadequate anesthesia" (2010: 177). "The most hotly debated subjects in pediatric care," Hardcastle notes:

> concerns whether infants are insensitive to pain. The presumption has been that young infants, especially premature newborns, cannot sense pain. As a result, no anesthesia or analgesics are used with heel lances, venipuncture, inoculations, and lumbar

punctures. Rarely is medication used with more invasive procedures, such as circumcision, bone marrow aspirations, or ligation
of a patent ductus arteriosus.

(1999: 196–97; see also Thernstrom 2010: 177)

The presumption of the insensitivity of infants is curious because it is
well documented that infants exhibit physiological responses to tissue
damage ("including sweating, increased heart and respiratory rates, the
release of adrenaline, crying, facial expressions, and motor behaviors"
[Hardcastle 1999: 197]).

Needless to say, this data about physiological responses of infants to
pain, given the additional data demonstrating that infant memory (and
therefore "experience"?) is significantly different from that of adult
humans, further complicate any conceptions of pain we try to formulate.
(Dr. Vertosick's patient complicates defining pain in a similar fashion
by confusing sensation and apprehension.) This is clear in Hardcastle's
conclusion that "early exposure to pain, whether remembered or not,
affects later experiences of and reactions to pain by altering the
developmental course of the nervous system. Infants, like other newborn
animals, learn to attach particular meanings or emotions or importance
to particular experiences in virtue of what is associated with those
experiences"; and she even goes on to speculate that "it looks as though
chronic pain and hypersensitivity can result from early acute pain
episodes, given how the neural receptors change" (1999: 199). That is,
these "events" of pain, whether or not they fit into any "perceptual"
notions of pain, become part of and shape the future experiential lives
of infants and children (by means of implicit memory). When such pain
events, moreover, are a result of the *social practices* of the healthcare
provided to young humans described here, the relationship between the
sensation and perception of pain that has been described throughout
this book is further complicated. (For this reason, as noted later, one
might fruitfully distinguish between biomedical "disease," the personal
experience of "illness," and the social event of "sickness" [see Boyd 2000;
Schleifer and Vannatta 2013: 3–7]). It is difficult to knowledgeably
speculate on why particular healthcare workers and the medical
profession as a whole found it so easy to presume the insensitivity of

infants to pain—it could be adherence to the assumption that pain is, by definition, part of (adult) consciousness; or to the more or less "physiological" assumption that infant humans were simply instances of "other newborn animals"; or to the assumption, as in Hemingway's story, that "screams are not important" (1970: 17); or to whatever conveniences in labor and expense such assumptions provide—but it is not difficult to judge that the behaviors that follow from such assumptions about pain must be considered, on some basic level, as *social* and, indeed, *political*.

Biases Related to Pain in Women

This social/political fact is even more notable in consistent social attitudes of healthcare workers and perhaps of society as a whole towards women in pain. One specific example of these attitudes towards women's pain is fibromyalgia (FMS). In recent years more than six million Americans have been diagnosed with FMS, and virtually all of them are women. FMS describes a "hodgepodge of symptoms . . . emanating from skeletal muscles and soft tissue almost anywhere in the body" (Fishman 2000: 215) represented by a collection of symptoms that includes widespread pain and a host of associated complaints, such as fatigue, headaches, sleep disorders, digestive disorders, depression, and anxiety (see Exhibit 6.2). Like chronic fatigue syndrome (CFS), which has been identified by most patients, physicians, and medical researchers as either the same or a sister disorder—it is another condition that predominates in

---

EXHIBIT 6.2

Here is a post from the internet where one sufferer of FMS describes her experience:

> My pain is stabbing, pulsing, pounding, radiating, cramping, tiring, ever-present, migrating, burning, almost always on my mind.

> I'm dizzy, nauseous, limping, tired, sleepy, fatigued, and hurting. At night, I am tossing and turning, stop breathing in my sleep and wake up and hurt all over – though I lay on a soft bed.

> ("All in My Head")

women—there are questions about the diagnostic legitimacy of FMS. Nevertheless, while medical accounts of chronic joint and muscular pain have existed for centuries, it is only since the mid-1970s that FMS has existed as a specific diagnosis. In 1990, the American College of Rheumatology established criteria for the classification of FMS: diagnostic criteria include the experience of widespread pain for at least three months in conjunction with subjectively reported tenderness in at least eleven of eighteen identified "tender points"; moreover, other possible causes for such pain must be disconfirmed. As this suggests, because there is no specific identified biomedical cause of FMS, there is great controversy of the "reality" of the condition itself:

> Some argue [FMS and other functional somatic syndromes such as CFS, irritable bowel syndrome and premenstrual syndrome] are linked by a shared but unknown organic pathology (Russell 1999); others maintain that these disorders are in whole or in part somatic presentations of depression or some other shared psychiatric illness (Manu 1998); still others argue that the specialty of the diagnosing physician determines which diagnosis is evoked to describe what is essentially a shared type of illness behavior.

Moreover, the fact that nearly all those diagnosed with FMS are women has led to predictable claims that FMS is the new clinical presentation of female hypochondriacity and/or hysteria (Barker 2002: 279–81; in her discussion she cites Goldenberg et al. 1990; Bohr 1995, 1996; Showalter 1997; Barsky and Borus 1999; Wessely, Nimnuan, and Sharpe 1999 as well as the citations within the quotation above).

FMS is a notable condition because its biomedical (physiological) uncertainty stands in sharp contrast to the subjective experiences of individuals diagnosed with FMS. In this, it is a stark example of the phenomena of the combination of personal certainty and social doubt that, as noted in earlier chapters, is a recurrent aspect of the experience of pain in general. Accounts of the pain and suffering caused by FMS are detailed, vivid, and often heart-wrenching, and one recurring feature in such accounts is that they often recount the social stigmatization and dismissal of the condition (see Exhibit 6.3). One powerful online blog (among many illness narratives online and in print) narrates the way that the syndrome seriously hampered social, family, and work life: the very fact that there was no specific diagnosis for a good period of time significantly compounded the pain and distress it created (see "All in My Head"). More generally, women diagnosed with FMS experience the fact that:

> while they recognize their symptoms as unambiguously real, those around them (family members, friends, employers, co-workers, and the medical profession) frequently do not. The outcome of this paradox for many with FMS is that they find themselves in an epistemological purgatory in which they question their own sanity precisely because of their certainty about the realness of their experience in the face of public doubt.
>
> (Barker 2002: 281)

EXHIBIT 6.3

Here is a post from the internet showing how social reactions complicate and intensify pain with anger and sadness:

> I am SICK AND TIRED of idiotic, moronic, asinine nurses and doctors trying to tell me that I don't feel what I feel. I'm tired of the condescending look they give me or the smile that says, "She's faking it." I hate that I feel terrible and sick and in pain all the time, and they write me off as being a hypochondriac or an attention-getter. They think they are almighty gods that know everything there is to know about me and my body. They feel that I'm a silly little girl that doesn't know pain, sadness, or suffering. Why can't they reach outside of their stupid little bubbles of medical knowledge and see that some things are beyond their reach? Why are they so STUPID? They think that they understand people automatically. They see me, and see the number of times I'm in the health center and automatically write me off. From the time they open my files, they don't listen to a word I have to say. And I'm sick of it. I'm sick and tired of not being believed. It's bad enough to feel miserable, but a broken heart just makes things so much worse. They are supposed to mend, not break.
>
> ("All in My Head")

Kristin Barker examines the social nature of this pain disease, following sociologists and others who distinguish between the biomedical (or physiological) nature of "disease," the social nature of "sickness," and the personal experience of "illness" (see Boyd 2000; Schleifer and Vannatta 2013: 3–7, although sociologists often describe the social nature of a condition "illness" without offering a term for its personal experience); and she analyzes the social creation of an "illness identity" in FMS. Since chronic pain, such as FMS, often does not command "cultural legitimacy," individual sufferers "work to remake their life worlds in the face of debilitating physical symptoms and medical and cultural marginalization." Barker argues that individuals suffering from FMS "construct a sense of themselves and of themselves in relation to others by situating themselves in public narratives [e.g., the FMS websites in Appendix II] to which they have access," and in the same action reconstruct a sense of their social selves and the meaning of their chronic pain (2002: 82–83). In her work, Barker demonstrates the ways that sufferers of FMS—in the face of the bias it provokes—are able to shape the boundaries and social meaning of their experiences of chronic pain.

The problem of FMS is a particular instance of larger social responses to chronic pain in women. The fact that far more women than men suffer from chronic pain (including FMS) calls for social and cultural explanations beyond Barker's analysis of the social construction of illness and social "illness identity" (see Exhibit 6.4). This fact calls for an explanation of social responses to illness as well as the social construction on the part of sufferers of illness. There is good evidence that men and women differ in their experiences of pain, although it is not clear whether these differences are a function of culture, social conventions, or physiology. (Most likely it is a combination of these factors.) Fishman notes that some "researchers seem to believe that women tend to have lower pain threshold and higher pain tolerance" while others have gathered evidence suggesting the opposite (2000: 21); and in a thoroughly documented argument Diane Hoffmann and Anita Tarzian demonstrate that "women experience pain more frequently, are more sensitive to pain, or are more likely to report pain" (2001: 19). Whatever the final analysis on this matter—I am strongly persuaded by the evidence and arguments of Hoffmann and Tarzian—there is good evidence that

---

EXHIBIT 6.4

In a recent article in the *New York Times*, Laurie Edwards noted that "an estimated 25 percent of Americans experience chronic pain, and a disproportionate number of them are women. A review published in the *Journal of Pain* in 2009 found that women faced a substantially greater risk of developing pain conditions. They are twice as likely to have multiple sclerosis, two to three times more likely to develop rheumatoid arthritis and four times more likely to have chronic fatigue syndrome than men. As a whole, autoimmune diseases, which often include debilitating pain, strike women three times more frequently than men" (2013: SR8).

---

men and women respond differently to pain medication: "one group of opioids (known as kappa-opioids) produces significantly greater analgesia in women than in men, probably reflecting a gender difference in pain-modulating circuits" (Morris 1998: 124; see also Hoffmann and Tarzian 2001: 13–15 for a thorough review of physiological differences). In any case, in the face of thoroughgoing study of the experience of pain in both men and women, Hoffmann and Tarzian conclude that:

> it seems appropriate that [women] be treated at least as thoroughly as men and that their reports of pain be taken seriously. The data do not indicate that this is the case. Women who seek help are less likely than men to be taken seriously when they report pain and are less likely to have their pain adequately treated.
>
> (2001: 19)

This is true for FMS and for chronic pain more generally. In fact, the evidence demonstrates this inequality of treatment in relation to pain. Men consistently receive more pain medication than women, both in consultation and post-operatively; they are more likely to be admitted to a hospital with chest pains; of people referred to pain clinics, men are more likely to be referred by general practitioners, women by specialists; on questionnaires, healthcare workers answered that they believed women were less sensitive to, more tolerant of, and less distressed by pain. In addition, less attractive people, men and women, were deemed to be in greater pain by healthcare workers; more attractive people were deemed to be more pain tolerant and simply more healthy, and insofar as women are socialized to attend to their appearance more carefully than men, they have their reports of pain discounted on this account (Hoffmann and Tarzian 2001: 17–18, 21). Some sociologists explain these differences in terms of women's endurance of childbirth, or more generally the assumption women have better coping mechanisms for pain; in terms of the necessity of treating men, who are the "breadwinners," more seriously; or simply by the fact that both doctors and nurses have greater reliance on "objective" evidence than self-reported pain. In any case, when men are judged to be forceful or aggressive, women are judged to be hysterical for the same behavior; and most generally healthcare workers assume more readily than with men that women's pain is psychogenic (Hoffmann and Tarzian 2001: 20–21). From this evidence, Hoffmann and Tarzian conclude that biases in relation to women's pain:

> have led health-care providers to discount women's self-reports of pain at least until there is objective evidence for the pain's cause. Medicine's focus on objective factors and its cultural stereotypes of women combine insidiously, leaving women at greater risk for inadequate pain relief and continued suffering. Greater awareness among health-care providers of this injustice, a readjustment of medicine's preoccupation with objective factors through educa- tion about alternative approaches, and scrutiny by quality and ethical reviewers within health-care institutions are necessary to change health-care providers' behavior and ensure that women's voices regarding treatment of their pain are heard.
>
> (2001: 23)

That is, mindfulness about the noxious qualities of pain *for all people* without distinctions of age and gender, can help make mitigation of pain more successful.

Torture

Of course, other social phenomena such as torture and sadism seek to increase rather than mitigate pain. This section focuses on torture but it should also be noted that sadism is also a social manifestation of pain, even though it takes place in interpersonal—usually sexual—relationships rather than in relation to larger social groupings. Sadism is touched upon in the discussion of pleasure and pain at the end of this chapter, but torture is an extreme manifestation of the larger social fact and experience of pain. Torture is the explicit political use of pain in order to obtain information, humiliate a person, and assert the absoluteness of state or social power. (It is important to notice how often pain lends itself to adjectives like *absolute, blank, overwhelming*, and their like.) In her powerful meditation of the nature of torture, *The Body in Pain*, published soon after the United Nations explicitly prohibited torture as illegal and unacceptable in 1984, Elaine Scarry describes the quality of pain in a powerful catalogue of the attributes of pain in relation to the "felt-experience of patient or prisoner." Scarry lists eight attributes of pain: (1) the "sheer aversiveness" of pain, (2) the experience of erasing and (3) asserting the agency of the producer of pain, (4) "an almost obscene conflation of private and public" as pain dissolves "the boundary between inside and outside," (5) "its ability to destroy language," (6) "its obliteration of the contents of consciousness," (7) "its totality" ("pain begins by being 'not oneself' and ends by having eliminated all that is 'not itself'"), and (8) "its resistance to objectification" and "representation" (1985: 52–56). These attributes are the direct opposite and negation of most of the elements of "personhood" that Dr. Eric Cassell argues are threatened and destroyed in suffering described in Chapter 5: the facts that personhood essentially includes the possession of conscious memory of the individual and familial past, exists within an external world of culture (including associations, roles, politics), is maintained within ordinary day-to-day activities, and encompasses more or less "unconscious" phenomena contributing to personhood (including ordinary bodily life, a contrary-to-fact "secret" or fantasy life, anticipations of worldly and "transcendental" futures)—all these things are overwhelmed in the *absolute* and *blank* experiences of pain. Scarry claims that pain destroys the opposition between outside and inside, the possibilities of conscious life and even *any* rhythms of life beyond the totalizing aversiveness of the felt moment of pain; and she claims that pain obliterates the human sociality of language and the sense of placement in the world that language—which entail inherited and acquired schemas—creates, even while pain produces an unarticulable sense of overwhelming agency, powers that overwhelm the self and personhood itself. These *qualities* of pain, Scarry argues, are organized into the "structure" of torture, which is comprised of three simultaneous phenomena: (1) the infliction of pain; (2) the objectification of the subjective attributes of pain (by which she means that pain "is to the individual experiencing it overwhelmingly present, more emphatically real than any other human experience, and yet it is invisible to anyone else, unfelt, and unknown"); and (3) "the translation of the objectified attributes of pain into the insignia of power" (1985: 51).

It is important that Scarry, for the purposes of her catalogue of eight attributes of pain, more or less equates the felt-experience of patient or prisoner—remember how Dr. Paul Brand suggests that hospital rooms are much like prison cells—because in doing so she more or less erases the *social* nature of pain (even while noting its *political* effects on victim and torturer) and focuses on its individual experience, the phenomenology of pain. But torture is a *social/political* institution: it has played "a central role in the evolution of law-state-society relations from ancient times to the early modern era" and thus emphasizes the ways in which the human experience and the physiological fact/event of pain has helped shape larger social formations (Hajjar 2012: loc 419; for a critique of Scarry's lack of political awareness, see Moyn 2013). In fact, in the founding of the United States the de-legitimation of torture with the prohibition of "cruel and unusual punishment" in the eighth Amendment to the Constitution is a significant instance of the serious questioning of traditional social practices and values that is part of the European Enlightenment of the seventeenth and eighteenth centuries. (Still, sociology has noted the fact that in American history "court-ordered punishments of people found guilty, no matter how cruel the methods might seem, were lawful" even if judicial *uses* of torture—i.e., "judicial torture" as distinct from "penal torture"—was outlawed [Hajjar 2012: loc 528–35].)

Unlike such sociological studies, Scarry examines torture in relation to the abstract notions of pain experience noted in her eight attributes of pain rather than the wider social significance of *politically inflicted pain*, even if she includes within the "structure" of torture the representation ("insignia") of social power. That is, in her wider study of pain, she never precisely argues, as Lisa Hajjar does in her sociological study, that:

> legally, severe pain and suffering constitute torture only if they are perpetrated against a person who is in custody by a person or people acting on behalf of some public authority or in an official capacity. This obviously applies to states and their agents, but it also could include non-state groups that exercise public power.
>
> (2012: loc 969–76)

Thus, Hajjar concludes that "many kinds of harmful practices might 'look like' torture, such as domestic violence, assault and battery, or even sadomasochistic sex, but they are not motivated by the purposes that constitute the international legal prohibition of torture" (2012: loc 969). Still, the sharp distinction she makes in her sociological study of torture between social and the personal contexts break down in the face of overwhelming pain. Hajjar notes that by many victims' accounts, sexualized torture—rape, sexual mutilations, forced nakedness, and other species of sexual humiliation—is the worst experience (2012: loc 1190), and in such experience the opposition between the social and the personal loses much of its force.

If, in fact, sexualized torture is the "worst," it goes a long way toward ratifying Cassell's definition of suffering as threatening and sometimes destroying "personhood." Moreover, it suggests that while Scarry most explicitly focuses on torture in *The Body in Pain*—perhaps, as Samuel Moyn recently argued (2013), because that book and much of Scarry's subsequent work were responses to the United Nations Convention against Torture and Other Cruel, Inhuman, or Degrading Treatment or Punishment in 1984—her book more fully explores the phenomenology of pain rather than torture. At the heart of her analysis is what

Moyn calls the "bizarre" notion that "the body in pain—physical distress of any sort—[is] the foundation of human creativity"; "in this way," Moyn concludes, "torture is the inverted likeness of the imagination; where the one destroys, the other fashions" (2013: 30). Scarry puts it this way:

> physical pain, then, is an intentional state without an intentional object; imagining is an intentional object without an experience-able intentional state. Thus, it may be that in some peculiar way it is appropriate to think of pain as the imagination's intentional state, and to identify the imagination as pain's intentional object.
>
> (1985: 164)

In philosophy "intentionality" and an "intentional state" describe the "property of being directed toward an object," e.g., to have something in mind; it describes forming a representation in mind and has nothing to do with having an intention (e.g., a "purpose"). This argument seems to suggest that pain is experience without an object of experience and imagination focuses on an object without "experiencing" it.

In arguing that pain has the "feel" of engagement with the world (i.e., that it is "intentional") but has no ("imagined") engagement with any part of or object in the world, she claims the experience of pain is *essentially* without an object:

> though the capacity to experience physical pain is as primal a fact about the human being as is the capacity to hear, to touch, to desire, to fear, to hunger, it differs from these events, and from every other bodily and psychic event, by not having an object in the external world. Hearing and touch are of objects outside the boundaries of the body, as desire is desire of *x*, fear is fear of *y*, hunger is hunger for *z*; but pain is not "of" or "for" anything—it is itself alone. This objectlessness, the complete absence of referential content, almost prevents it from being rendered in language.
>
> (1985: 161–62)

This argument assumes that pain is, in its very nature, simply *perception/ experience*; it offers no sense of pain "imagined" as related to a *sensory fact/event*, "localizable" both within the sensory system and in relation to a stimulus (e.g., my *toe* hurts). Yet at the same time torture, in her literary/phenomenological analysis of pain experience, seems to assume that the pain gives rise to an "experience" (if this is possible) of *pure sensation*, without meaning (as in religion), without context (as in medicine), concentrated on the narrow subject "experiencing" such pain, reduced simply to "the body in pain." In Scarry's analysis of torture, then, the complexity of pain as it has been described throughout this book precipitates out, so to speak, into separate parts, the exaggeration of perception, the exaggeration of sensation, which are then collapsed into the pure experience of objectless sensation. In Hajjar's sociological account of torture, pain is described as sensation without much analysis of experience. These focuses on "experience" and "data" nicely demonstrate the complementary work of culture and science (see Appendix I).

Pain and Religion

In her study of the phenomenology of pain, Scarry examines the relationship of pain to religion. The self-flagellation of the religious ascetic, she argues:

> is not (as is often asserted) an act of denying the body, elimin-
> ating its claims from attention, but a way of so emphasizing the
> body that the contents of the world are cancelled and the path
> is clear for the entry of an unworldly, contentless force. It is in
> part this world-ridding, path-clearing logic that explains the
> obsessive presence of pain in the rituals of large, widely shared
> religions as well as in the imagery of intensely private visions,
> that partly explains why the crucifixion of Christ is at the center
> of Christianity, why so many primitive forms of worship climax
> in pain ceremonies.
>
> (1985: 34)

Similarly, in his book examining the relationship of religion to suffer-ing, John Bowker describes "the crucial importance in any religion of the account it gives of suffering." "To talk of suffering," he argues, "is to talk not of an academic problem but of the sheer bloody agonies of existence, of which all men are aware and most have direct experience. All religions take account of this; some, indeed, make it the basis of all they have to say" (1970: 2). This section glances at two examples of religious traditions focusing upon our shared human experiences of pain. The first is the visionary experience of Saint Teresa of Avila, a sixteenth-century Catholic—a Spanish mystic—who wrote extensively on the relationship between her personal pain and her visionary experience; and the second is the collective experience of Tamil Hindu pilgrims literally pursuing pain in an annual pilgrimage in honor of the deity Ayyappan. The Tamil experience makes clear what is implicit in the pain experiences of Teresa: that however "personal" religious experiences are, they are also social and cultural. Religion, as explicitly as any human institution or practice, attempts to comprehend the brutish bloody agonies of human life under the categories of significance and purpose. We have seen Dr. Paul Brand, a devotedly religious man, do this in trying to account for pain in the world that he believes was created by a loving God in his book, *The Gift of Pain*. (It should be noted that besides her visionary experience, Teresa had a strong social life: she was an effective and important organizer of Spanish institutions for nuns.)

In her work, Teresa attempts to meditate upon "the most secret things [that] pass between God and the soul" (1946: II, 201, 202) in relation to pain and suffering in order to describe the ways that the physiological *fact* of pain can be *phenomenally* gathered up into a meaningful whole of religious significance and a powerful sense of transcendental subjectivity (i.e., a sense of self outside worldly contexts). That is, Teresa combines the experience of pain and religious vision: she suffered from "unbearable" pain in her nerves, intense headaches, fainting spells, and likely suffered from epileptic seizures (Hatzfeld 1969: 84–85; Atran 2002: 189; see also Trimble 2007: ch. 7 for the "neurotheology" of epilepsy). In her *Life*, written in 1565, she offers the most famous of her descriptions of intense visionary religious experience tied to an experience of excruciating pain, one that occasioned Bernini's famous sculpture *The Ecstasy of Saint Teresa* (1652) and Richard Crashaw's poem, "A Hymn to the Name and Honor of the Admirable Saint Teresa" (1646) about a generation after her canonization in 1622 (she died in 1582). In her vision, she is visited by an angel in whose hands she saw:

a long golden spear and at the end of the iron tip I seemed to see a point of fire. With this he seemed to pierce my heart several times so that it penetrated to my entrails. When he drew it out, I thought he was drawing them out with it and he left me completely afire with a great love for God. The pain was so sharp that it made me utter several moans; and so excessive was the sweetness caused me by this intense pain that one can never wish to lose it, nor will one's soul be content with anything less than God. It is not bodily pain, but spiritual, though the body has a share in it—indeed, a great share.

(1946: I, 192–93)

Afterwards "during the days that this continued," Teresa writes that she "had no wish to see or speak with anyone, but only to hug my pain, which caused me greater bliss than any that can come from the whole of creation" (1946: I, 193). David Morris emphasizes the "blended, eroticized, mystical pain" both in Teresa's narrative and Bernini's sculpture (1991: 132), but more to the point are the ways that Teresa's experience instantiates Scarry's sense of the totalizing power of pain: "pain begins," Scarry writes, "by being 'not oneself' and ends by having eliminated all that is 'not itself'" (1985: 54). For Teresa the pain is "sharp" but becomes quickly (immediately?) something she cannot imagine being without. Elsewhere, Teresa repeatedly describes her religious experience as a kind of out-of-body experience, very much in accordance with the

---

EXHIBIT 6.5

Maureen Flynn describes Teresa's pain as "the one human quality that she carried with her. To be fully embraced by her Bridegroom she had to destroy first the animal passions and physical sensations ruling the organic body. Pain constituted proof that her human nature was being purified. She affirmed suffering along the passage to psychic purity because it suggested that she was nearing her destination to an immaterial presence. In this theology of ecstasy every tinge of corporeality implied the beginning of the end of temporal existence. Physical sensation of the most unbearable sort indicated that the hand of God was tearing from the soul its worldly inclinations" (1996: 273).

ways that Scarry describes the "objectlessness" and ego-destroying effects of pain (see Exhibit 6.5). In Teresa's experience, pain–as we have seen, the *most* emphatic sensation—becomes ghostly, immaterial, other-worldly. In this understanding, as Ariel Glucklich describes it, "pain, in short, unmakes their profane world and leads the mystics to self- and world-transcendence" (2001: 42; he goes on to compare phantom limb pain to visual hallucinations).

That is, in his analysis of what he calls "sacred pain," Glucklich describes such religious experiences in terms closely related to the "secret life" Cassell numbers among those aspects of personhood that are threatened or destroyed to produce suffering. Specifically, Glucklich describes a sense of "personhood" in terms of the "body-self template" Melzack has posited under the term "neuromatrix" encountered in Chapter 3, which led Marni Jackson to assert that "pain is not an invasive, alien force or a learned response but part of the map of who we are. Pain should not surprise us (a point of view that Buddhists have been teaching for some time)" (Melzack 1993: 621–27; Glucklich 2001: 54–57; Jackson 2002: 76). In this way, the work of "sacred pain" is to *realize* personhood by creating a sense of empowerment but also, and most strikingly, by diminishing "the subjective experiencer" to the point of creating a subject absorbed into a higher power, what Teresa figures as her "Bridegroom" (Glucklich 2001: 98, 59). For Teresa—and for the experience of "sacred pain" more generally—the pain that is felt, such as when Teresa glimpsed the image of the suffering Jesus or when she feels impaled by an angel, also provokes the experience of religious pleasure, that of self-displacement and self-transformation discussed later, *without ceasing to be terrible pain*. Still, pain experience—even the pain of disembowelment—is "objectified" as a feeling and element integrated into a whole, now transcendental self, "completely afire with the great love for God" (1946: I, 193). In this experience, Teresa combines ecstasy and pain: Morris notes that Teresa is a "visionary figure in whom rapture and pain seem strangely united" (1991: 131). In her *Life*, as we have seen, she describes her vision of an angel plunging a spear deeply within her. In her visionary expression, that depth encompasses several of Cassell's attributes of personhood combined with Scarry's attributes of pain in realizing "sacred pain." This combination can help us to see the ways that the physiological fact of pain can be taken up by—rather than destroying—the phenomenological experience of personhood.

If Teresa's experience of pain is also an experience of most fully experiencing a sense of transcendental personhood, then the Tamil Ayyappan pilgrimage that anthropologist Valentine Daniel describes does the opposite. In this annual pilgrimage participants suffer from lacerated feet, blisters, scorching sunshine in a barefoot forty-mile trek. "Sooner or later," Daniel (who himself underwent the pilgrimage) writes, "different kinds of pain begin to merge." He describes three kinds of pain: pain as part of *perception*, and particularly perception of meanings in the world, such as Brand's description of leprosy patients apprehending themselves to be "uniquely cursed by God" (Brand and Yancey 1997: 271); pain as a dyadic threat to personhood, a one-on-one *oppositional* "experience of *pain* [that] makes one acutely aware of oneself (ego) as the victim, and the outside (undifferentiated as roots, stones, and hot sand) as the pain-causing agent"; and pain as simple and pure *sensation*, in which "pain stops having a causative agent, and ego is obscured or snuffed out because it has nothing to contrast itself with or stand against." In this last condition—the *experience* of pain, which is the aim of the pilgrimage—he notes that:

> there is a "feeling" of pain, of course, but it is a sensation that has no agent, no tense, and no comparative. One does not know whence the pain came, how it is caused, or whether it is more or less intense than the pain a moment or an hour ago; for there is no before or after. Pain is the only sensation belonging to the eternal present.
>
> (Daniel 1987: 267–68)

Here, in the Tamil Ayyappan pilgrimage the experience of *suffering*—of threat to personhood—is replaced by the struggle with the "sheer averseness" of pain (to use Scarry's term), and that in turn is replaced by a pure sensation of pain, without either self or struggle. (This is very different from the pure experience of pain in torture Scarry describes, where self is reduced to body *experiencing* pain.) In this, the *perception* of pain is overwhelmed by *sensation*. More specifically, Daniel claims that the Tamil pilgrim strives:

> to move away from the world of theories and laws . . . [and dissolves] the rules and theories that classify "the other" into just one other (in the case of the pilgrimage, *pain*), which looms out against the self . . . [in order to reach a place] where the "other" is experienced in such immediacy that it is no longer clear where the self ends and the other begins.
>
> (1987: 244)

When this occurs, "pain itself [is] conquered by love" (1987: 257). "Several pilgrims seemed to believe, however," Daniel observes, "that after a while, pain, having become so intense, began to disappear. In the words of one pilgrim from my village, 'At one moment everything is pain. But the next moment everything is love (*anpu*). Everything is love for the Lord'" (1987: 269). In the Tamil pilgrimage, Daniel notes that "pain, to begin with, is multiple and differentiated"—the pain of toe and heel blisters, of the weight of his backpack, of headache in the baking sun (see 1987: 272)—but "with time, the various kinds of pain merge into a unitary sensation of pain" that is then replaced by "love" (1987: 274; for a semiotic examination of this phenomena upon which this discussion is based, see Schleifer 2009: 145–59). Pain is also conquered by love in Teresa's visionary experiences, but in her experience, unlike the Tamil experience, the subject of experience is not simply— or altogether—gathered up in love without active subjects and objects of love. That is, these two ways in which religion *engages* pain focus upon and emphasize, respectively, pain conceived as *perception* (Teresa) and pain conceived as *sensation* (Tamil pilgrims). In both cases, the urge is to transform what I have called the "facticity" of pain—its sheer aversiveness—into something that fits within a social and communal religious system of purpose and value.

Pleasure and Pain

As well as in religious significance, pain has been taken up as a determining factor in moral social judgments. In the late eighteenth century, Jeremy Bentham, founder of utilitarianism, published *Introduction to the Principles of Morals and Legislation*. In that book, he set forth the opposition between pain and pleasure:

> Nature has placed mankind under the governance of two sovereign masters, *pain* and *pleasure*. It is for them alone to point out what we ought to do, as well as to determine what we shall do. On the one hand the standard of right and wrong, on the other the chain of causes and effects, are fastened to their throne.
>
> (Bentham website)

In his argument pain and pleasure are opposite extremes on the same spectrum. Close to 100 years later, the British economist William Stanley Jevons attempted to create a mathematical model for economics by assuming that "pleasure and pain, of course, are opposed as positive and negative quantities" (1866: website). He goes on to argue that "infinitesimal" quantities of both pleasure and pain can be measured to form a "calculus" of economic values by means of which economic values and actions can lend themselves to mathematical analysis. In our time, such a calculus of pleasure/pain has been formalized—in economics,

---

EXHIBIT 6.6

In the late nineteenth century, the great American economist, Thorstein Veblen, vehemently opposed such a calculating, mathematical economics of the opposition of pleasure and pain, noting that social relations always entail *social* power relationships, which the *individual* calculations of pleasure and pain do not take into account. The pleasure/pain calculus of the neoclassical economists of the late nineteenth century (including Jevons), he believed, assumed what he calls the "hedonistic conception of man" understood as "a lightning calculator of pleasures and pains, who oscillates like a homogeneous globule of desire of happiness under the impulse of stimuli that shift him about . . . but leave him intact" (1898: 73). As we have seen, Moyn makes a parallel critique of Scarry's analysis of the (individual) body in pain, which he argues fails to engage with possible collective (political) action in relation to torture.

philosophy, sociology—as "rational choice theory," which assumes, as Jevons and Bentham do, that pleasure and pain are simple opposites and, as such, subject to rational calculation of one sort of another (see Exhibit 6.6).

Yet our experiences of pleasure and pain are not so easily opposed to one another. Moreover, a close examination of pleasure can help us more fully appreciate the experience of pain itself, including its social aspect. We saw earlier in Chapter 3 Scarry's remarkable description of pleasure in her comparison of pain and touch—the difference, though she does not say so, between the work of A-beta fibers and A-delta fibers. She distinguishes a finger cut by a thorn and feeling—almost caressing—a woven cloth, and in the latter case she describes how the woman who feels the cloth "experiences the sensation of 'touch' not as bodily sensations but as self-displacing, self-transforming objectification" (1985: 166). She goes on to argue that this feeling is called *pleasure*, "a word usually reserved either for moments of overt disembodiment or, as here, moments when acute bodily sensations are experienced as something other than one's own body" (1985: 166; note this description in relation to Teresa's and Tamil pilgrims' experiences of pain). She further describes pleasure as "a condition associated with living beyond the physical body, or experiencing bodily sensations in terms of objectified content" (1985: 355). In this account, pleasure is not so much the opposite to pain as it is something else, a different *kind* of experience altogether that neither is *localized* in term of a particular part of the body ("my *finger* hurts") nor so overwhelming that the content of experience "blanks out" everything else.

In his study of the relation of pleasure to meaning in the time of European Romanticism (i.e., the turn of the nineteenth century), the sociologist Colin Campbell describes pleasure in a different way that might further clarify a sense of the experience of pain. He asserts that the experience of pleasure is distinct from the gratifications of need (though such gratification often takes the form of the relief of pain). It is notable that his chief example of need is hunger, which, as we know, is painful in its effect. Pleasure, he argues, organizes itself in a very different way from objects of need. "Objects," he writes:

possess utility or the capacity to provide satisfaction. It is, in this sense, an intrinsic attribute of real things: food can relieve hunger, clothes provide warmth, houses shelter, people affection. Pleasure, on the other hand, is not an intrinsic property of any object but is a type of reaction which humans commonly have when encountering certain stimuli. Pleasure is not even a property of stimuli, but refers to the capacity to react to stimuli in a certain fashion. To search for satisfaction is thus to engage with real objects in order to discover the degree and kind of their utility, whilst to search for pleasure is to expose oneself to certain stimuli in the hope that they will trigger a desired response within oneself. Hence, whilst one typically needs to make use of objects in order to discover their potential for satisfaction, it is only necessary to employ one's senses in order to experience pleasure, and, what is more, whereas an object's utility is dependent upon what it is, an object's pleasurable significance is a function of what it can be taken to be.

(2005: 61)

Campbell's analysis of pleasure can easily be understood as taking up the same terms and understanding used to describe pain when pain is conceived of as *experience/perception* rather than a fact/event of *sensation*; in fact, his description can easily help us understand the phenomenon of religious pain/pleasure of Teresa. That is, the strict opposition of pleasure and pain—dating back to Bentham and his followers, such as Jevons—is a problem insofar as it does not take into account the complexity of pain as both *sensation and perception*. Like the Marquis de Sade, Bentham's contemporary, it takes pain to be simply a physiological fact/event. Scarry, as we have seen, focuses most fully on pain as simply a noxious perception/experience.

Pleasure, Paul Brand also notes, "is more perception than sensation"; "each square inch of skin contains thousands of nerves for pain and cold and heat and touch, but not a single pleasure cell" (Brand and Yancey 1997: 68, 289). Rather, he says, pleasure emerges as a by-product; and "even more than pain," it is "an interpretation only partly dependent on reports from the sense organs" (Brand and Yancey 1997: 289). But pain itself, as we have seen throughout this book, is also only partly dependent on reports of sensation and itself can be seen as a "by-product." Thus, Valerie Gray Hardcastle reports one research trial where subjects were given one of three consent forms by which they agreed to participate in an experiment that might (1) result in intense but harmless pain; (2) result in pleasure; or (3) in which no experience was mentioned. They did a mathematical problem and then put their finger in a vibrating machine. Subjects who signed the form describing pain reported the vibrations as "stinging" or "burning" and ranked the experience as painful; those who signed the form describing pleasure reported a "tingling" sensation and ranked the experience as pleasurable; those with the form without mention of any expected experience described it as "vibrating" and ranked it as neither painful nor pleasurable. Hardcastle concludes that "belief and expectation play an important role in how we experience pain," and notes this is particularly true for chronic pain (1999: 170–71).

The complexity of pain as both sensation and perception, as it has been described throughout this book, is perhaps most clear in the oddness of finding pleasure in pain in the cases of sadism and masochism. These are psychological conditions, psychosexual disorders in which pleasure is gained by inflicting pain on others or receiving pain oneself. There have been both elaborate psychological and sociological analyses of these phenomena—the issue of interpersonal power relations as they are connected to aspects of sexual fulfillments recurrently comes up in these discussions—yet the seeming self-contradictory combination of pleasure and pain might best be examined in relation to the history of the term *sadism*, coined by the German psychiatrist Richard von Krafft-Ebing in 1890. Krafft-Ebing took the term from the Marquis de Sade, who wrote about deriving sexual pleasure from inflicting pain in the late eighteenth century. (Krafft-Ebing also coined the term *masochism* from another writer, Leopold von Sacher-Masoch, who wrote about deriving sexual pleasure from having pain inflicted upon oneself.) A look at the Marquis de Sade should contribute to the examination of experiences of pain pursued in Part II of this book.

David Morris argues that the notion of pain articulated by Sade in the late eighteenth century—at the same time that torture was taken to be cruel and unusual punishment by the new American republic—created a new conception of pain in history, one that is complexly bound up with the European Enlightenment. For Sade, Morris notes, when characters in his novels:

> talk about pain as an event of hollow nerve fibers and neural fluids, they invoke a vision in which mind and soul have disappeared into matter. Sadean eroticism thus belongs to the same world of material fact as the modern medicine that has increasingly come to understand humankind as little more than unusually complex machinery in need of occasional repairs.
>
> (1991: 232)

Moreover, Morris goes on to argue that as well as creating a foundation of morals and law, as Bentham thought the opposition of pleasure and pain did, "Sade shows how reliance on pleasure and pain can just as easily undermine every principle of law and morality." Morris concludes that:

> the blankness, the anythingness of pain, especially its power to summon up experience ultimately inaccessible to language, its power to evoke and engage ambiguities too slippery for even the slickest libertine [i.e., "sexually wanton"] reasoners: these are among the most radical meanings with which Sade endowed the mechanical rush of animal spirits through hollow, fibrous nerves.
>
> (1991: 237, 238)

The blankness of pain that Morris, following Emily Dickinson, describes is the fact that the fact/event/experience of pain can be taken up individually, socially, and politically as a way of understanding and experiencing the world. In this way, pain might well be, as many have argued, one of the essential elements of human life that include, as I mentioned at the very beginning of this book, joy, community, happiness, and even pleasure. Its experience, as these chapters suggest, is at once personal and social, a *horizon* of possibilities of experience that shapes all parts of our lives.

PART III
LIVING WITH PAIN

7

CARETAKERS AND SUFFERERS
DEALING WITH PAIN

Pain can only be treated successfully if it's treated. Even with
modern technological wonders, too many patients feel more pain
than necessary because it is either overlooked or not made a
priority. Effective treatment starts with recognizing the need for
treatment and taking action. Too many patients are afraid to
complain. And, too, many doctors and nurses are either unaware
of their patients' pain or disregard it . . .

Nowhere is Hippocrates' directive to "Study the patient rather
than the disease" more critical than in pain medicine, *because
pain is a symptom of a patient's suffering.*

—Dr. Scott Fishman, *The War on Pain*
(2000: 24–25)

Definitions of Pain

Throughout, this book has presented various definitions of pain. It has
presented several vivid representations of pain, such as the narrative
description of the young man with leprosy in Chapter 1 or Emily
Dickinson's metaphorical description of pain as simply "blank" in
Chapter 5; it has described pain in relation to other sensory systems,
such as sight, hearing, and touch; and it has offered several working

Figure 7.1 Dealing with Pain

definitions of pain simply in terms of the "work" it does, such as unpacking Dr. Scott Fishman's notion of pain as an "alarm" system. These three kinds of definition correspond to what philosophers describe as three different ways we define elements of experience and cognition, three ways of grasping and shaping meaning in the world (see Bridgman 1927; Robinson 1972).

Exemplary Definition

A first kind of definition offers simply an example of the phenomenon subject to definition. That is, this definition simply *points* to an object or experience in the world. Thus, many dictionaries will offer an iconic image—a simple drawing—of an oboe as part of the definition; and when Emily Dickinson describes pain as containing "an Element of

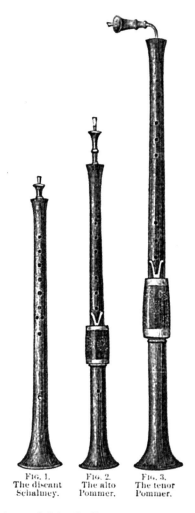

FIG. 1.
The discant
Schalmey.

FIG. 2.
The alto
Pommer.

FIG. 3.
The tenor
Pommer.

Figure 7.2 Encyclopedia Images Defining the Oboe

Blank," she is offering a metaphorical *example* of what pain feels like, an example of what it is. Thus an exemplary definition of pain simply "points to" its quality (e.g., 6 on a pain scale of 0 to 10) in order to convey its meaning. In his study, *Listening to Pain: Finding Words, Compassion, Relief,* Dr. David Biro offers extended analyses of metaphors that describe pain in this way: metaphors of pain as a *weapon/agent* that *does* something to the sufferer, as when patients talk of pain as "stabbing" or "shooting"; pain as a *mirror*, when the fact/

experience of pain allows the sufferer to observe and understand what is happening to her ("the gloomy sky that shares our sadness"); and pain as an *X-ray*, that allows it to be figured as some "interior landscape" of body and meaning ("a forest fire sweeping down the . . . piping network of my digestive tract") (2010: 16, 132, 142, 170). *Exemplary Definition* corresponds to the traditional conception of the humanities described in Appendix I as "mere description."

Aristotelian Definition

A second kind of definition, systematically set forth by Aristotle, defines something in terms of its *genus* (the larger class in which it belongs) and its *species* (the "specific" elements it possesses that distinguishes it within that class). Thus, an *oboe* is a woodwind instrument (i.e., its genus) that functions by means of a double reed (i.e., specifically distinct from the single reeds of clarinets or the lack of reeds in flutes). It can also be distinguished from the *bassoon* as a "double-reed instrument with a certain tonal range" (in which case "double-reed instrument" is the genus, and the tonal range defines the species). In a similar fashion, Valerie Gray Hardcastle (and many who approach pain from the point of view of a fact/event that allows the precisions of "law-like" [nomological] analysis as opposed to the perception/experience that Dickinson attempts to capture) defines pain as a sensory system (i.e., its genus, that includes other sensory systems such as sight and hearing sensory systems) that is also distinct from those other systems in terms of the *quality* of its sensation (e.g., the unpleasant sensation of pain vs. the pleasant sensation of touch) and the *objects* of its sensation (e.g., noxious somatic feelings in the body vs. colors or sounds in the world) (see Exhibit 7.1).

Operational Definition

A third kind of definition was developed very late, in the twentieth century after Einstein's work on the Special Theory of Relativity. In his initial discussion (1905: Einstein website), Einstein gives a *working* definition of "simultaneity," stating that two things are simultaneous when seemingly at the same moment we see the train pull into the station and see the clock noting it is 7 pm. Here, instead of defining *simultaneity* as "two events or facts [genus] that occur at the same instant of time

---

EXHIBIT 7.1

It is interesting to note that the opposition between exemplary and Aristotelian definitions can be seen in the history of torture. Lisa Hajjar notes that one reason torture was so widespread in medieval Europe was "the fact that *circumstantial evidence* was not admissible for serious crimes" with the consequence that confession was imperative. "For example, if a man was found holding a bloody knife next to a dead body but no one had seen him stab the other person, the bloody knife was circumstantial evidence and he could not be convicted of murder unless he confessed. Consequently, torturing people to get them to confess to crimes became a key tool of law and order. Most medieval European states relied on torture to investigate serious crimes within their jurisdiction" (2012: loc 490–79). Unlike an exemplary definition, which is basically an assertion of meaning—*that* is an oboe!—an Aristotelian definition is *indirect*: it follows a logic of genus and species, which includes inferences from a part (species) to a whole (genus): a bloody knife in someone's hand and a cut body (parts) leads to the inference of an act of murder (whole).

[species]" (an Aristotelian definition), or simply pointing to the fact of "the train's arrival and the clock's long is hand touching 12 and its short hand is touching 7" (an exemplary definition), an operational definition sets forth how the phenomenon to be defined *works*. In Einstein's case he focuses on the element of light necessary in order to *see* the clock and the train at the same moment. His point was that light travels at a finite speed, and if the clock were placed far enough away from the station by the time the light from the clock allowed one to see the time as 7 pm, the actual time on the far-away clock would be different from the time conveyed by light moving at a finite speed (say, 7:05 pm). This *operational*—or as Dr. Scott Fishman says, "functional"—definition does not create an attested exemplary or logically "essential" definition as in the first two modes of defining objects, but rather analyzes *how something works* and describes what *results or actions* the defined object creates in the world. (In this way, this definition functions in the manner suggested in Chapter 1 that the humanities and cultural studies function, to lead to *action in the world*.) In 1927 in analyzing Einstein's work, the American philosopher Percy Bridgman coined the term *operational*

definition to distinguish the *kind* of definition Einstein set forth from those of example and genus/species (1927).

These three modes of definitions—and the three different definitions of pain they give rise to—are of the upmost importance for our understanding of how to deal with pain. The analysis of pain set forth in this book (see especially Appendix I) has argued that the "examples" of exemplary definition are not as immediate as they seem, but entail schematic forms of *attention and expectation* inherited from our environments, cultures, and even the long history of evolution. Thus, when we attend to the image of an oboe, seemingly immediately apprehended, we *expect* that it is not a weapon of combat, a convoluted stick to beat someone with, but rather a musical instrument. That is, the seeming *immediate* sense of the broader sense of what something is—its genus—is, in fact, mediated by cultural forms of attention and expectation. Similarly, the seeming "scientific" precision of Aristotle's definition also entails (assumed) schemas of attention and expectation: while Aristotelian definition makes the shared qualities of a genus and the distinguishing elements of a species explicit (they are implicit in exemplary definitions), both the general genus and the specifications of differences are also conditioned by schemas of expectation and attention (as in *changing* genus: oboe as woodwind; oboe as double-reed instrument).

Both exemplary and Aristotelian kinds of definitions—broadly speaking, those of culture and those of nature—nicely correspond to conceptions of pain emphasizing perception and sensation respectively. But neither is particularly efficacious in *dealing* with pain, particularly from the vantage of healthcare. One (exemplary) aspect of pain that has been repeatedly noted is that pain experience is absolutely real from the vantage of the subject who feels the pain, while it is subject to doubt almost to the same degree from the vantage of someone who is not experiencing it. As Elaine Scarry asserts, pain "is to the individual experience it overwhelmingly present, more emphatically real than any other human experience, and yet is almost invisible to anyone else, unfelt, and unknown" (1985: 51). That is, while we seemingly immediately accede to an exemplary definition—that *is* an oboe!—the declaration of pain doesn't work so clearly. Thus, in the case of "exemplary" presentations of pain, the healthcare worker can acknowledge or distrust a patient's report of pain, and the substantial attention toward strategies for ascertaining the truthfulness of patient reports described in discussions of pain in the face of drug addiction, hypochondria, and other alternative possibilities (in Meier, Biro, ordinary responses to fibromyalgia, and even in the important work of Dr. Scott Fishman presented in this chapter) is striking.

Similarly, in the context of chronic pain, an Aristotelian definition of pain in relation to other sensory systems is hardly practically useful in treating pain, precisely because it assumes the *alarm sensation* of pain is the defining quality of pain (its genus), and therefore defining pain in this manner does not create possibilities of accounting for chronic pain as a phenomenon in which the pain itself is the "disease". That is, chronic pain fails to properly "alarm," but it does not suspend sensation. In other sensory systems the failure of the system *eliminates* sensation (as blindness or deafness eliminates light sensations or compressed air sensations); but chronic pain is a dysfunction of a sensory system that nevertheless "reports" sensation. As such, despite the fact that pain is, in part, "sensory," it does not function like a sensory system. For this reason, given an Aristotelian understanding of pain—which is seemingly more "objective" (and "natural") than an asserted ("subjective"; "cultural") example—a healthcare worker will have the tendency to distrust a patient's report of pain that does not fit into the genus of "alarm": if the specific goal of pain sensation is to account for pain sources in the same way that the specific goals of sight and sound sensations are to account for sources of those phenomena in the environment (as an Aristotelian notion of genus suggests), then pain reports can simply be defined as "psychogenic," which is to say something that is "subjective" and does not fit within systematic definition of "real" pain. Time and again in reading narratives about pain I have found such denial in the examples of physicians who, failing to find a physiological basis for pain, transform their enthusiastic hopes to help their patients into distrust of patient ("exemplary") reports of pain.

The Functional Definition of Pain

An operational definition of pain functions differently. Thus, in *Listening to Pain*, Dr. Scott Fishman systematically calls for a "functional" definition of pain rather than some universal definition. That is, he argues that since claims of pain are always "subjective" and, for that reason, not verifiable, healthcare workers should approach the pain patients bring to the clinic in terms of how that pain works (or "functions") in their lives. Specifically, he argues, instead of solely focusing on the *experience* of pain (1) by asking patients to describe the pain they feel on a scale of 0 (no pain) to 10 (worst pain imaginable) or (2) by focusing on the *fact/event* of pain (e.g., my toe aches, my head aches)—these two accounts follow from exemplary and Aristotelian modes of defining phenomena—healthcare workers most efficiently should focus on *what the pain does* in terms of limiting patient's functioning in the world. Thus he argues that:

> *the direct sensation associated with pain is not the only important variable and may not be the most important feature of the overall presentation of pain.* The real key to understanding pain and formulating an effective treatment plan is to look beyond the pain sensations to how those sensations are eroding a patient's quality of life. Specifically, how is the patient's pain affecting his or her *functioning* in daily life?
>
> (2012: 40)

In defining pain in this way, he is negotiating between definitions of pain as sensation and as experience. "Measuring the intensity of emotional pain," he argues, "is as subjective and elusive as quantifying physical pain. Measuring the amount of functional loss caused by pain, however, is an objective and quantifiable calculation" (2012: 39).

That is, Fishman argues that pain reports are necessarily *subjective*, that they essentially present exemplary definitions of the pain involved and, as we have seen, such exemplary definitions of pain are particularly problematic because of the huge difference between the experience of the sufferer and the listener. However, he goes on, to understand pain in terms of the functions it inhibits (which is an operational definition of pain) creates *objective* goals that can organize *action in the world*:

> If, over the course of the day, [patients'] pain varies from a 4 to an 8 out of 10, I want to know what they can do when their

pain is a 4 that they can't do when it is an 8. What meaningful activities are no longer possible and how were those activities lost over time? Once I can establish the level of functional losses in relation to pain, I can begin to envision possible goals for reclaiming lost functions.

(2012: 32)

The goals he envisions are *specific*: "return to playing golf, ability to make love again, returning to gainful employment or volunteer work, driving a car, attending a child's sporting event, or leaving the reclining chair in the living room and sleeping in their beds at night" (2012: 32). His book is addressed to physicians, and he ends his presentation of his operational definition of pain with a second-person admonition to doctors:

In place of unverifiable and subjective pain symptoms, you can base your assessment and treatment plan on objectively record-able goals and outcomes. Instead of relying exclusively on the patient reports and all the difficulties inherent in that model, you can collaborate with your patients to set clear and objective goals and a system for verifying progress on them.

(2012: 56)

In this, Fishman is emphasizing what is crucial to an operational definition of pain, namely the *collaboration* of patient and physician in defining pain and developing ways to deal with it. An exemplary definition is solely based upon the (unverifiable) report of the patient; an Aristotelian definition is based upon a scientific/objective logic of understanding possessed by the physician. But an operational definition encompasses both. Thus, the physician needs "to believe in the patient" in order to create functional goals that are set "collaboratively between patient and doctor"; that are "realistic and achievable"; that are "meaningful to the patient"; and that are subject to verification (for both patient and physician) (2012: 35, 57). "The important point," he concludes, "is that patients are in charge of their therapy and part of their responsibility is to provide you with evidence of their progress"

(2012: 76). One implication of the collaboration between patient and physician implicit in an operational definition of pain is the replacement of the problematic term "compliance" in descriptions of patient responsibility. Dr. Arthur Kleinman describes how "compliance" is a marker for a particular coercive quality in patient–physician engagements: "It's a lousy term," he says. "It implies moral hegemony [a hierarchy of power]. You don't want a command from a general, you want colloquy" (cited in Fadiman 1998: 261). Similarly, Fishman suggests that "the term 'adherence' may be preferred to the more traditional 'compliance' because of the possible connotations of coercion in the term 'compliance'" (2012: 67) and the implication that a patient "adheres" to a mutually agreed-upon plan. A second implication of an operational definition of pain and a functional definition of treatment is physician—and, more generally caretaker—satisfaction in their work with patients in pain. As Dr. Vannatta and I argue in *The Chief Concern of Medicine* (2013), this is an added benefit to patient–physician collaboration in facing pain and suffering. Such collaboration takes the overwhelming burden of responsibility off the shoulders of healthcare workers—and caretakers

---

EXHIBIT 7.2

In an interview, Dr. Rita Charon defines *empathy* as a combination of cognitive and emotional *understanding*—a kind of "recognition" of the humanity, and the human suffering, of another person. "'Empathy,' she has said, 'is the method, or the tool, that gets you toward engagement. Empathy is that ability to recognize the plight of another person and to be moved by it. Empathy does not require that I have experienced what the patient is experiencing.' [Rather, it requires the "recognition" of] the patient's plight . . . Such recognition also entails being willing to invest one's self emotionally in the patient and her story in the direction, as Charon says, towards engagement. When the physician and patient engage in this manner, they experience a deeper, more meaningful relationship—one built on mutual understanding, trust, and a kind of identification. This engagement describes rapport and it is established through the development of empathetic recognition and understanding" (Schleifer and Vannatta 2013: 160; for the whole interview, see Vannatta, et al. 2005: ch. 2, screen 35).

more generally—and makes the treatment of pain a shared responsibility and, in fact, deeply meaningful. (See Exhibit 7.2.)

The Operational Definition of Addiction

Before turning to the implications of a functional definition of pain for the treatment of pain—the issue of healthcare workers, caretakers, and patients themselves *dealing* with pain in this concluding chapter—we should examine a second operational definition that Fishman delineates in *Listening to Pain*, namely an operational definition of addiction. Although he is not as explicit in presenting an operational ("functional") definition of addiction as he is for pain, nevertheless his recurrent return to the question of addiction in relation to pain-relieving drugs in a book whose audience is practicing physicians indicates the strong concern many physicians and healthcare workers have concerning the addictive "side effects" of opioids. The recent book by Barry Meier, *A World of Hurt*, mentioned in Chapter 4, that traces both the widespread abuse of opioids and, more strikingly, their *inefficiency* in responding to the terrible conditions of chronic pain, is both a source and symptom of this worry about pharmaceutical treatments of pain by physicians and others. Fishman's operational definition of addiction—like his functional definition of pain—is an important antidote to the double problem of under-medication and over-medication with opioids. Again, it cuts through the opposition between pain or addiction as a fact/event—the sensational definition of pain and the physiological definition of addiction presented in Chapter 4—and pain or addiction as a perception/experience; it cuts through the opposition between the (seeming) scientific/objective logical analysis of an Aristotelian definition and the (seeming) experiential/subjective presentation of an exemplary definition.

Fishman is very anxious to articulate a *functional* definition of addiction. He describes one patient who was using drugs without obtaining any real *functional* benefit. That is, his patient claimed to "feel better," yet none of the functional measures and goals that he articulated in relation to his chronic pain changed in any significant way. Still, Fishman notes that:

> I believe clinicians must be very careful with the label "addict."
> I draw the distinction between a "chemical coper" and an addict.

Many people are "chemical copers" either with legal or illegal drugs. They use drugs to cope with life and remain relatively healthy and functional despite, perhaps, being chemically dependent on a drug. Addicts, on the other hand, have a disease that impairs their ability to control or modulate their use of a drug that is causing them dysfunction. They also continue to crave and use the drug *despite* the dysfunction. For an addict, enough is never enough.

(2012: 45–46)

Later he notes that:

patients with addiction have a disease that is stimulated by the drug that they are addicted to, resulting in dysfunction. Patients in pain are dysfunctional because of their pain, and the drugs that relieve their pain should improve their function. If you focus on function, these outcomes are diametrically opposite to each other.

(2012: 81)

In this definition, Fishman is reluctant to make chemical dependency the defining feature of drug addiction. Instead, as with his definitions of pain and pain relief, he measures the definition of addiction in terms of the *outcome* of drug use in relation to pain and the functions that pain destroys in the life of the patient. As mentioned earlier, such a definition looks beyond the "objective" truths of Aristotelian definition and the "subjective" truths of asserted pain experiences to develop a program of *action in the world* in relation to what pain and addiction *do*. In fact, even in cases of clear drug abuse, Fishman suggests that the goal of pain relief often requires more than a punitive policy of "one strike and you're out": "the patient who flunks a urine test, runs out of a prescription early, or complains aggressively should not simply be kicked out and denied medication." Instead, he recommends listening to the patient, in collaboration with her, to "find a functional-based solution" (2012: 104–05).

Dealing with Pain

The mechanism for *enacting* treatment implicit in an operational definition of pain—and, for that matter, of addiction—begins, as Fishman stresses, with *careful listening* and *careful observation*. First and foremost—it is a shame this must be said—healthcare workers and those who share their lives with people in pain must simply *acknowledge* the fact of pain itself. As Fishman notes:

> Research bears this out: patients who feel that they have good rapport and communication with their doctors [and caretakers] consistently report better treatment outcomes and higher levels of well-being and satisfaction. This body of research speaks to the central truth about treating pain: *simply acknowledging your patient's pain can have profound therapeutic effects.* Just knowing that a caregiver believes their pain exists and wants to help alleviate it makes it easier for patients to endure their pain. In fact, it actually reduces the intensity of their pain.
>
> (2012: 5)

Moreover, what caretakers should listen for—and watch for in relation to what is *not said* by patients—is what Dr. Vannatta and I describe as the *concern* of the patient: what his pain means to him and how its treatment works for him. (This is particularly important in relation to opioids.) To elicit such meaning, as we suggest in *The Chief Concern of Medicine*, calls for particular strategies. The first strategy is careful listening, specifically listening for:

- what we call "hot words" such as "money," "life partner," "scared," "boss," etc. (Fishman asks physicians to attend to what "a patient might casually mention" [2012: 22]);
- the "unspoken" emotions the patient brings with her pain, such as the fear, anger and sadness discussed in Chapter 5 (Fishman notes that "patients in pain have many reasons to be angry, argumentative, mistrustful, anxious, and depressed" [2012: 87]);
- the difference ("anomaly") between the patient's explicit goals and their behavior;

- any possible culture impediments to communication (language, religious/spiritual assumptions, gender, class, age, etc.).

A second strategy is careful questioning, including question:

- specific pain-related questions, such as: "do you find yourself constantly irritable?"; "do you find sleep difficult?" (a question Lous Heshusius gratefully answers when one physician who "gets it" asks); "have you lost your appetite?"; "do you find it difficult to relax?";
- any euphemisms and notable metaphors; and
- open-ended "functional" issues as Fishman recommends, such as "is there anything you can't do now that you could do previously?"; or "what is it that you're going to do on this medicine that you can't do now?" (2012: 33, 42; see Exhibit 7.3).

Like Dr. Fishman, in our book we argue that part of the work of healthcare entails *active* listening and questioning that implicitly acknowledge the reality of patients' pain.

That is, like Fishman, we argue that the work of healthcare includes attending to the patient's *concern*, what the patient thinks her pain means to her life. We believe that making the chief concern explicit —by making its articulation an explicit part of the patient's chart (i.e., "The History and Physical Exam" physicians record)—functions to move the discussion between patient and physician into another category: from symptoms of biomedicine to concerns embedded in the

---

EXHIBIT 7.3

These strategies are organized in checklists. In *The Chief Concern of Medicine*, especially Appendix 2, Dr. Vannatta and I present checklists for patient–caretaker interactions, and although he does not use the term, Fishman repeatedly creates checklists of strategies of action for physicians. For the functional utility of checklists in healthcare—a form of knowledge leading to action emphasized throughout this book—see Gawande 2010.

patient's experience expressed in narrative. Moreover, this is also a movement from knowledge to action. Getting the job done in medicine entails discovering—which is to say, *negotiating with the patient*—what "health" and "illness" mean in a particular situation and establishing a pragmatic plan of action that grows out of those situational definitions. This is Dr. Fishman's overriding point, born of years of engagement with and treatment of people in intractable pain. In medicine this is accomplished by eliciting and attending to the story—the narrative— patients bring with their illness. When the occasion of disease and illness is pain, these narratives can be particularly cryptic and terse. But all illnesses have elements of distress—suffering and pain—that make it particularly important for healthcare workers and caretakers to listen with care and engagement. (For a thoroughgoing discussion of the role of narrative in medicine, see Charon 2006.)

At the end of *The Chief Concern of Medicine*, Dr. Vannatta and I present a short vignette that took place in his practice. In this story, the patient involved is filled with fear, which is to say his situation is that of suffering more than the sharp sensations of pain. Yet the vignette describes the way a caretaker can deal with distress—pain and suffering—and it also suggests ways that patients themselves can come to think about articulating as clearly as possible what their pain *means* to them. A young woman resident physician saw a new patient in the clinic. He had come because he was unhappy with his previous physician. He had presented to the previous doctor with ascites (fluid in the abdominal cavity) and a CAT scan of the abdomen had revealed cirrhosis of the liver. The resident concentrated on the patient's physical examination, CAT results, and blood tests. When Dr. Vannatta as the attending physician asked her what the patient wanted them to do that the other physician had not done she did not have an answer.

As attending physician, Dr. Vannatta recognized in this account that important parts of the patient's narrative were missing, namely (1) exactly why did the patient not return to the first doctor; and (2) what specifically was his chief concern about this cirrhosis (what brought the patient to the doctor in the first place). Moreover, he also recognized in the account something about the young resident physician as well: that she was troubled about her encounter with her patient without quite knowing what was wrong. What was wrong, he sensed, although she did not quite articulate it either to him or to herself, was a vague understanding that she—like the first physician whom the patient had left—was somehow not getting the job done. She was troubled—again, without quite understanding it—that, for all her knowledge and clear perception of the cause of this man's problem, she hadn't found the means of caring for him. Vaguely, there was something missing in her encounter with this patient that led her to believe that there was something wrong with how she was doing her job.

Dr. Vannatta entered the room and after introducing himself, asked the patient what he understood the problem to be. The patient answered "cirrhosis" and further explained that it was causing the fluid. He then asked the patient "What is your primary concern about this cirrhosis?" The patient said, "Well, I don't want to die of it." By making the patient's chief concern explicit, Dr. Vannatta elicited what the patient thought the diagnosis of cirrhosis meant—probable death. This was a simple interchange, but in it the conversation had shifted from a discussion of symptoms and diagnoses to one of meaning and action. The patient was able to express his fear of death and this allowed Dr. Vannatta (together with his patient) to focus on the patient's concern and, most important, it allowed him to begin a negotiated action plan. Without this new strategy of interaction the young resident physician was getting ready to tell the patient the same thing the first doctor told him; she was getting ready to focus on the ascites and ignore the patient's chief concern. Dr. Vannatta explained to the patient the several possible causes of cirrhosis—hepatitis B, hepatitis C, genetics, nonfatty liver disease, autoimmune problems, alcohol—and discussed the patient's alcohol consumption. The patient denied being an alcoholic, despite the fact that he drank to excess on a daily basis. Dr. Vannatta told his patient that, in fact, cirrhosis is serious and life-threatening, but the patient could attend to his concern about the fatal nature of his condition by his actions. "Cirrhosis usually does not get better," he told his patient, "but it can get worse. And we can work out something you can do to give us a chance that it doesn't get worse." He had a sense that the first physician the patient had seen, like the young resident, never moved from biomedicine to a functional plan (with its implicit narrative) and never gave himself or his patient the chance to move from the category of factual knowledge to the category of action (adapted from Schleifer and Vannata 2013: 359–61). Similarly, as Fishman suggests, in encountering a patient suffering from chronic pain, a caretaker should explicitly ask *what the pain is taking from her life* (which is to focus on the *life concern* chronic pain gives rise to). This focus on concern—what the patient wants in terms of verifiable activities—makes *collaborative* action rather than uncovering knowledge the heart of pain care.

The Care of Patients

The care-full concern described here can be pursued by patients as well as caretakers. Throughout her own harrowing narrative of pain and its understanding, *The Pain Chronicles*, Melanie Thernstrom occasionally describes the philosopher Friedrich Nietzsche, who suffered painful gastrointestinal distress throughout his life—probably due to syphilis, from which he finally succumbed—that it left him sleeplessly nauseous for more than 200 nights per year for many years. Specifically, she quotes Nietzsche in his final stage of syphilis, consumed by burning nerve pain declaring that:

> Throughout life I have seldom known respite from pain, having had at least two hundred days of suffering each year. . . . I have given a name to my pain and call it 'dog.' It is just as faithful, just as obtrusive and shameless, just as entertaining, just as clever as any other dog—and I can scold it and vent my bad mood on it, as others do with dogs, servants and wives.

In her own illness, Thernstrom found Nietzsche's image "fatuous": "was he trying to cheer himself up by pretending he was master? Was he not in pain when he wrote it? *Was he kidding?*" (2010: 39).

Here she dismisses Nietzsche, yet towards the end of her book, she focuses on dogs again in relation to "learned helplessness." Near the end, she interviews Sean Mackey, the head of the Stanford pain service, who told her that early in his career he "realized how much of the treatment [of pain] involved trying to reverse learned helplessness"—to rally patients "out of the despair ingrained by years of unremitting pain and to cajole their minds to offer up the analgesic that minds themselves are capable of creating" (2010: 305). Learned helplessness has been demonstrated in experiments with dogs, she notes: two-thirds of dogs that are regularly shocked, when put in a setting in which they can avoid pain by simply jumping over a low barrier, will not even try, and simply lie on the ground and whine. But then she asks, "what about the one-third of dogs who leap away?", and notes that "pain upsets and destroys the nature of the person who has it—but not always" (2010: 306).

In another book entitled *Listening to Pain* (that shares its title with Fishman's book, though it aims at a patient audience rather than a physician audience), Dr. David Biro traces the classes of metaphors mentioned earlier in this chapter: pain as an active agent doing something to you; pain as a mirror, where sufferers can find a sense of meaning in their terrible experience; and, pain as an X-ray that lends insight into a person's inner values. He explores these metaphors from literature and other sources to describe the way that metaphor allows a person "to express his experience, in the etymological sense of pushing it outward (*expremere*)." He gives one example from James Joyce's autobiographical novel, *A Portrait of the Artist as a Young Man*—a text we encountered in Chapter 1—which describes the way that an image of a train in a tunnel "mirrors" his chief character's pain. Such expression, Biro says, allows Joyce to gain "some control over [his pain] (by naming it) and [to be] no longer alone, both of which help to relieve his pain" (2010: 69–70). In his discussion of the nature of suffering, Dr. Eric Cassell makes clear—as Nietzsche did—the relief latent in a sense of control that such metaphors ("train," "dog") creates. "People in pain," Cassell writes, "frequently report suffering from pain when they feel out of control, when the pain is overwhelming, when the source of the pain is unknown . . . or when the pain is apparently without end." But he notes that "suffering can often be relieved *in the presence of continued pain*, by making the source of the pain known [and] changing its meaning" (1991: 36). Similarly, although Thernstrom dismisses it, Nietzsche is attempting to create a strategy for himself as a sufferer of pain to assert some kind of control, to *unlearn* the helplessness that chronic pain occasions. Moreover, the functional definition of pain described in this chapter allows caretakers and sufferers themselves to create and pursue active responses to pain beyond the apparent helplessness that suffering inflicts.

That is, with these understandings and actions, by themselves or in concert with caretakers, patients find the ability to do for themselves what Dr. Fishman and Dr. Vannatta and I have described: to integrate the factual knowledge—the science and "events"—of pain with a program of action that organizes itself around the *meanings* of even the most terrible experiences of pain and suffering in relation to life activities. Such integration can allow caretakers of every sort—physicians, nurses, family, friends, and patients themselves—to face the terrible and over-whelming facticity of pain with a human response, individual and collective. Such care-full resistance to pain answers the brutality of the world with, as Margaret Mead suggests, the work of civilization. The brutality of the world is most manifest in the pain to which we are always subject. As we have seen throughout this book—as we have all seen in our lives—pain feels sovereign, brutish, destructive of the everyday goodnesses we share with one another, of the world of values we create, together and individually, for ourselves and our communities. The archeological "signs of healing" Mead describes show "that someone must have cared for the injured person—hunted on his behalf, brought him food, served him at personal sacrifice" (cited in Brand and Yancey 1997: 275). Together, as caretakers and sufferers, we must continue to show care, patience, and understanding—and in so doing develop focused action—for the pain we see, for the pain we feel.

Appendix I
Pain, Science, and the Humanities

The complex understanding of pain as event and experience integrates science and culture. That is, if the sciences pursue *facts* and *events* and, more than factual events, universal *laws* that govern phenomena and their behaviors, then the humanities and cultural studies are centrally concerned with *experience*, and particularly, as suggested most explicitly in Chapters 1 and 7 but also throughout this book, with experience leading to action. Science, at one extreme, pursues the strict causal laws of the "nomological" (or "law-governed") sciences, while the social sciences—epidemiology is a fine example—pursue *patterns* and *trends* to be found in data, rather than strict formulas of nomological science. (See Exhibit A.1.) Still, both focus predominantly on facts and events.

Nomological science, since the time of René Descartes and Isaac Newton in the seventeenth century, has pursued "certainty," as Descartes described it, and discovered certainty in mathematical representations of facts and events. That is, science, at this extreme, aims at discovering the *necessary and sufficient conditions* that govern the existence of phenomena and their behaviors (facts and events); it aims, at this extreme, to articulate universal laws. This is the meaning of "nomo-logical" or "law-like" science, and its chief representative example can be seen in the universal formulas of mathematical physics that describe the necessary and sufficient conditions governing physical facts and

---

EXHIBIT A.1

Nomological Science (sometimes called **Deductive-Nomological Science**) is a model of "scientific" understanding that pursues "law-like" explanations that are logically and universally true.

Epidemiology is a model of understanding that pursues patterns, causes, and effects of the conditions of health and disease—including the "dis-ease" of pain—in a defined population. Epidemiology does not articulate a "law" that explains phenomena everywhere with a universal causal explanation, but seeks to accurately describe observed data that may suggest patterns, causes, and effects in a local environment.

---

events. For such sciences, empirical facts and events are "commensurable" across different particular cases, which means that different instances can be taken as equal: *any* falling object will behave like any other, or any neuron like any other ("the neurons that make up the brain are essentially identical across all animals in the kingdom" [Hardcastle 1999: 63]). Throughout her book *The Myth of Pain*, Valerie Gray Hardcastle repeatedly notes that all pain is the "same": "all pains are physical and localizable and . . . all are created equal" (1999: 7). Moreover, she assumes that there is "a lawful connection" between a mental state (such as the experience of pain) and physical events or objects that give rise to it, particularly neurological events (1999: 40; throughout *Pain and Suffering* I have referred to Hardcastle because in her philosophical work [1995, 1999] she cites numerous scientific studies of pain drawn from cognitive psychology, neurophysiology, and clinical neurology—some of which I include in the bibliography—which follow the model of nomological scientific explanations).

Along with the nomological sciences, there are also other scientific pursuits that are less logically rigorous in their goals, empirical and explanatory sciences such as epidemiology (mentioned above), evolutionary biology, or the social sciences in general. (In Chapter 6, I focus on sociological studies of pain.) Like evolution, most of these social studies pursue retrospective science that cannot *predict*, as nomological science can, future facts and events (Gould 1989). Nomological science can do this because its formulas (for instance, $e = mc^2$ or $f = ma$) *universally* apply so that if we are given the mass (m) and acceleration (a) of an object, we can always calculate and predict its force (f). In distinction to such nomological science, evolution and, in a different register, other social sciences are historical sciences, which make sense of facts and events in retrospect. In this, they describe *sufficient but not necessary conditions* governing facts and events. That is, evolution pursues not universal formulas but *retrospective explanation*: it is not "necessary" that the mammalian eye evolved—one can imagine a different kind of sensory-perceptual system—but having come into existence, one can explain it, retrospectively, as the product of a long history of "sufficient" advantageous adaptations. In a sense, this is still, weakly conceived, a law-like science insofar as it is governed by the "law" of natural selection—itself confirmed by precise empirical study (see Weiner 1995 for a fine empirical study of natural selection)—but such a law is the *basis* rather than the *goal* of its scientific endeavor.

Against these scientific projects, the work of the humanities and cultural studies is different. The humanities and cultural studies do not seek the necessary and sufficient formulas of nomological science governing facts or events or the sufficient explanations of facts and events in evolutionary or epidemiological science. Rather, the humanities focus on *experience* rather than facts and events. Thus, in a pioneering work on the cultural study of pain David Morris argues—in a passage that directly contradicts Hardcastle's assertion that "all pains . . . are created equal" (1999: 7)—that "what we feel today when we are in pain . . . *cannot* be the same changeless sensations that have tormented humankind ever since our ancestors crawled out of their caves" (1991: 4). To make this argument, as we have seen throughout this book, Morris focuses on particular timely *experiences* of pain, which he suggests are not always commensurable with other experiences of pain.

The assumption of the incommensurability of the objects of the humanities and cultural studies has a long history. That is, it was long assumed that "humanistic, as opposed to natural, phenomena are non-recurrent and for that very reason cannot, like natural phenomena, be subject to exact and generalizing treatment." For this reason, it was assumed, the humanities—and cultural studies more generally—simply pursued "mere description, which would be nearer to poetry than to exact science" (Hjelmslev 1961: 8–9). Such a traditional view suggests that rather than analyzing phenomena in ways that focus on their exact and generalizing treatment, the humanities and cultural studies focus on phenomena as they are *simply* (which is to say, uniquely and unmediatedly) experienced. There is good reason to disagree with this conclusion because there is good evidence that it is possible to treat human experience in exact and generalizing ways by studying the *schemas of experience* just as the social sciences treat *patterns and trends of social life* in exact and generalizing ways and the nomological sciences treat *commensurable physical and biological phenomena* in exact and generalizing ways. (Throughout, this book has described schemas that condition experiences of pain.) Moreover, there is good reason to believe that such study—perhaps most clearly in cultural studies and the medical humanities—is more interested in functional definitions and *practical action* in relation to its knowledge than in discovering and articulating more or less *universal knowledge and laws* in scientific study. In this book the practical implications of our understandings of pain for engaging with people suffering from pain is repeatedly emphasized.

This alternative view of cultural studies, which fully allows the *integration* of the sciences and culture, can most clearly be discerned in the study of human pain. That is, pain is a fact and an event: various instances of pain, in fact, are *commensurable* facts and events that lend themselves to exact and generalizing treatment. But in its very nature pain is also a particular *experience*. In this, the combination of commensurable fact and seeming unique and non-recurring experience makes the study of pain a defining site for the integration of the sciences and humanities/cultural studies. In recent work (see Schleifer 2009, 2009a, 2009b, 2012, Schleifer and Vannatta 2011, 2013) I have argued that it is mistaken to understand the humanities as simply "mere description." Rather, the *experience* that the humanities study—and, in fact, human experience more generally—is not immediate and unique, even if it feels itself to be so, but rather governed and conditioned by *schemas of experience* and *neurological subroutines*, the same way this book demonstrates that the event and experience of pain themselves can be understood as exact and generalizing in the *formulas and explanations* of science and also in the *schemas of experience* that the humanities study. Such schemas are either learned from personal and vicarious experience or inherited in neurological subroutines that have been evolutionarily adaptive. Both inherited and acquired schemas function to allow us to anticipate future action (Steen 2005; Schleifer and Vannatta 2013: 14–26, 95–104); that is, the functional purpose of these schemas is to prepare us for action in the world. (In Chapter 7, I examine in detail a *functional* definition of pain that prepares caretakers and sufferers for action in the world.)

The study of pain and suffering suggests, then, that the humanities do not (always or even predominantly) study unique and non-recurring phenomena, but rather they study *necessary but not sufficient conditions* of experience itself; they study frameworks or *schemas* that govern and condition what "feels" like immediate experience. In doing so, this study suggests that the *felt immediacy* of perception and experience—including the defining case of the perception and experience of human pain—can be understood as *mediated*. Such mediation is effected by means of evolutionary adaptive motor, sensory, and cognitive "subroutines" or "subsystems" designed to adapt the individual and the species to a dangerous world by means of creating and ordering recurring patterns of experiential phenomena. And, on more local temporal levels than the deep history of evolution, such adaptive and cognitive mechanisms conditioning and governing experience are effected ("mediated") by particular *schemas* of experience learned throughout a lifetime from our parents and from the wider culture that tutor us in shared conventions and assumptions in order to make many aspects of our experience what they are. Both of these understandings call into question the simple notion of "immediate experience."

Appendix II
Online Resources Focused on the Nature and Treatment of Pain

The following is a list of online resources focused on the nature and treatment of pain that might prove useful for pursuing specific issues and questions raised in this book. (While the following addresses were correct at the time of publication, they should be easily traceable even if the precise address changes.)

American Academy of Pain Management: www.aapainmanage.org
American Academy of Pain Medicine: www.painmed.org
American Chronic Pain Association: www.theacpa.org
American Medical Association Pain Management (Online Series): www.ama-assn.org/ama/pub/physician-resources/pain-management.page
American Medical Association: www.ama-assn.org
American Pain Foundation: www.painfoundation.org
American Pain Society: www.ampainsoc.org
American Psychological Association: www.apa.org
American Society for Action on Pain: www.druglibrary.org/schaffer/asap
American Society of Addiction Medicine: www.asam.org
Brief Pain Inventory: www.mdanderson.org/education-and-research/departments-programs-and-labs/departments-and-divisions/symptom-research/symptom-assessment-tools/brief-pain-inventory.html
Fibromyalgia Support Group: www.mdjunction.com/fibromyalgia
Hyperbole and a Half's "Better Pain Scale": www.hyperboleandahalf.blogspot.com/2010/02/boyfriend-doesnt-have-ebola-probably.html
Initial Pain Assessment Tool: www3.mdanderson.org/depts/prg/bpi.htm
International Association for the Study of Pain: www.iasp-pain.org

Life with Chronic Pain: A How-to Guide: www.everydayhealth.com/blog/life-with-chronic-pain

McGill Pain Questionnaire: www.npcrc.org/files/news/mcgill_pain_inventory.pdf

MD Junction Support Groups: www.mdjunction.com

National Center for Health Statistics: www.cdc.gov/nchs

National Fibromyalgia and Chronic Pain Association: www.fmcpaware.org

National Pain Foundation: www.painconnection.org

Pain Treatment Topics: www.pain-topics.org

Pain.com: www.pain.com

PainACTION: www.painaction.com

Partners Against Pain: www.partnersagainstpain.com

Psychology of Pain: psychologyofpain.blogspot.com

The Mayday Pain Project: www.painandhealth.org

The Pain Web: www.thepainweb.com

Stories of a Girl with Fibromyalgia: www.allinmyhead.webs.com

UCLA History of Pain Project: unitproj.library.ucla.edu/biomed/his/pain.html

University of Wisconsin Pain and Policy Studies Group: www.painpolicy.wisc.edu

Visual Analog Scale: www.painedu.org/Downloads/NIPC/Pain%20Assessment%20Scales.pdf

WebMD Pain Management Health Center: www.webmd.com/pain-management/default.htm

Wong-Baker FACES Pain Rating Scale: www3.us.elsevierhealth.com/WOW

BIBLIOGRAPHY

"All in My Head: Stories of a Girl with Fibromyalgia." Blog: http://allinmyhead. webs.com/ (accessed on June 5, 2013).

Atran, Scott, *In Gods We Trust: The Evolutionary Landscape of Religion*. New York: Oxford University Press, 2002.

Barber, J. and D. J. Mayer, "Evaluation of the Efficacy and Neural Mechanism of a Hypnotic Analgesia Procedure in Experimental and Clinical Dental Pain," *Pain*, 4 (1977): 41–47.

Barker, Kristin, "Self-Help Literature and the Making of an Illness Identity: The Case of Fibromyalgia Syndrome (FMS)," *Social Problems*, 49 (2002): 279–300.

Barsky, Arthur J., and Johnathon F. Borus, "Functional Somatic Syndrome," *Annals of Internal Medicine*, 130 (1999): 910–21.

Benedetti, Fabrizio, *Placebo Effects*. New York: Oxford University Press, 2008.

Bentham, Jeremy, *Introduction to the Principles of Morals and Legislation*. Available at www.econlib.org/library/Bentham/bnthPML1.html (accessed on June 20, 2013).

Biro, David, *Listening to Pain: Finding Words, Compassion, and Relief.* New York: Norton, 2010.

Bohr, Thomas, "Fibromyalgia Syndrome and Myofascial Pain Syndrome: Do They Exist?" *Neurological Clinics*, 13 (1995): 365–84.

——, "Problems with Myofascial Pain Syndrome and Fibromyalgia Syndrome," *Neurology*, 46 (1996): 593–97.

Bowker, John, *Problems of Suffering in the Religions of the World*. Cambridge: Cambridge University Press, 1970.

Boyd, Kenneth, "Disease, Illness, Sickness, Health, Healing, and Wholeness: Explore Some Elusive Concepts," *Journal of Medical Ethics: Medical Humanities,* 26 (2000): 9–17.

Brand, Paul and Philip Yancey, *The Gift of Pain: Why We Hurt and What We Can Do About It*. Grand Rapids: Zondervan Publishing House, 1997.

Bridgman, Percy Williams, *The Logic of Modern Physics*. New York: Macmillan, 1927.

Campbell, Colin, *The Romantic Ethic and the Spirit of Modern Consumerism*. London: Alcuin Academics, 2005. (Reprint of the 1987 edition.)

Cassell, Eric, *The Nature of Suffering and the Goals of Medicine*. New York: Oxford University Press, 1991.

Charon, Rita, *Narrative Medicine: Honoring the Stories of Illness*. New York: Oxford University Press, 2006.

Damasio, Antonio, *The Feeling of What Happens: Body and Emotion in the Making of Consciousness*. New York: Harcourt, 1999.

Daniel, E. Valentine, *Fluid Signs: Being a Person the Tamil Way*. Berkeley: University of California Press, 1987.

Daudet, Alphonse, *In the Land of Pain* (ed. and trans. Julian Barnes). New York: Alfred A. Knopf, 2002.

Derruchat, P. and D. Baveux, "Correlational Analysis of Explicit and Implicit Memory Performance," *Memory and Cognition*, 17 (1989): 77–86.

Dickinson, Emily, "Pain—Has an Element of Blank," *Poetry X*, ed. Jough Dempsey. August 25, 2004. Available at http://poetry.poetryx.com/poems/2901/ (accessed on July 1, 2013).

Domangue, B. B., C. G. Margolis, D. Lieberman, and H. Kail, "Biochemical Correlates of Hypnoanalgesia in Arthritic Pain Patients," *Journal of Clinical Psychiatry*, 46 (1985): 235–38.

Donald, Merlin, *Origins of the Modern Mind: Three Stages in the Evolution of Culture and Cognition*. Cambridge: Harvard University Press, 1991.

Edelman, Gerald, *Bright Air, Brilliant Fire: On the Matter of the Mind*. New York: Basic Books, 1992.

——, *Wider Than the Sky: The Phenomenal Gift of Consciousness*. New Haven: Yale University Press, 2005.

Edwards, Laurie, "The Gender Gap in Pain," *New York Times*, March 16, 2013, SR8.

Einstein, Albert, "On the Electrodynamics of Moving Bodies," 1905. Available at www.casavaria.com/hotspring/2008/05/21/123/einsteins-special-theory-of-relativity-the-original-paper-1905/ (accessed on July 21, 2013).

Fadiman, Anne, *The Spirit Catches You and You Fall Down: A Hmong Child, Her American Doctors, and the Collision of Two Cultures*. New York: Noonday, 1998.

Ferrier, David, *Functions of the Brain* (second edition). New York: Plenum Press, 1886.

Fishman, Scott (with Lisa Berger), *The War on Pain*. New York: Quill, 2000.

——, "Clinical Commentary," in Lous Heshusius, *Inside Chronic Pain: An Intimate and Critical Account*. Ithaca: Cornell University Press, 2009, pp. 131–48.

——, *Listening to Pain*. New York: Oxford University Press, 2012.

Flynn, Maureen, "The Spiritual Uses of Pain in Spanish Mysticism," *Journal of the American Academy of Religion*, 64 (1996): 257–78.

Freeman, W., and J. W. Watts, *Psychosurgery in the Treatment of Mental Disorders and Intractable Pain*. Oxford: Blackwell, 1950.

Gawande, Atul, *A Checklist Manifesto: How to Get Things Right*. New York: Metropolitan Books, 2010.

Glucklich, Ariel, *Sacred Pain: Hurting the Body for the Sake of the Soul*. New York: Oxford University Press, 2001.

Goldenberg, Don L., Robert W. Simms, A. Geiger, and Anthony L. Komaroff, "High Frequency of Fibromyalgia in Patients with Chronic Fatigue Seen in a Primary Care Practice," *Arthritis and Rheumatism*, 33 (1990): 381–87.

Gordon, B., "Preserved Learning of Novel Information in Amnesia: Evidence for Multiple Memory Systems," *Brain and Cognition*, 7 (1988): 257–82.

Gould, Stephen Jay, *Wonderful Life: The Burgess Shale and the Nature of History*. New York: Norton, 1989.

Grahek, Nikola, *Feeling Pain and Being in Pain* (second edition). Cambridge: MIT Press, 2001.

Gureckis, Todd and Robert Goldstone, "Schema," in *The Cambridge Encyclopedia of the Language Sciences*, ed. Patrick Colm Hogan. New York: Cambridge University Press, 2011, pp. 725–26.

Hajjar, Lisa, *Torture: A Sociology of Violence and Human Rights*. New York: Routledge, 2012 (cited with Kindle location numbers).

Han, Ji-Sheng, "Acupuncture and Endorphins," *Neuroscience Letters*, 361 (2004): 258–61.

Hardcastle, Valerie Gray, *Locating Consciousness*. Amsterdam: John Benjamins Publishing Company, 1995.

——, *The Myth of Pain*. Cambridge: MIT Press, 1999.

Hatzfeld, Helmut, *Santa Teresa de Avila*. New York: Twayne Publishers, 1969.

Hemingway, Ernest, "Indian Camp," in *In Our Time*. New York: Scribner's, 1970, pp. 15–21.

Heshusius, Lous, *Inside Chronic Pain: An Intimate and Critical Account*. Ithaca: Cornell University Press, 2009.

Hilts, Philip, *Memory's Ghost: The Strange Tale of Mr. M. and the Nature of Memory*. New York: Simon and Schuster, 1995.

Hjelmslev, Louis, *Prolegomena to a Theory of Language*. Trans. Francis Whitfield. Madison: University of Wisconsin Press, 1961.

Hoffmann, Diane and Anita Tarzian, "The Girl Who Cried Pain: A Bias Against Women in the Treatment of Pain," *Journal of Law, Medicine, and Ethics*, 29 (2001): 3–27.

"How You Feel Pain," Mayo Clinic www.riversideonline.com/health_reference/Nervous-System/PN00017.cfm (accessed on October 13, 2013).

Iacoboni, Marco, *Mirroring People: The Science of Empathy and How We Connect with Others*. New York: Picador, 2009.

IASP (International Association for the Study of Pain), definition at www.iasp-pain.org/AM/Template.cfm?Section=Pain_Definitions (accessed on June 30, 2013).

Jackson, Marni, *Pain: The Fifth Vital Sign*. New York: Crown Publishers, 2002.

Jeffers, Robinson, "The World's Wonders," in *The New Pocket Anthology of American Verse*, ed. Oscar Williams. New York: Pocket Books, 1955, pp. 243–44.

Jevons, William Stanley, "Brief Account of a General Mathematical Theory of Political Economy," *The Journal of the Royal Statistical Society*, 29 (June 1866): 282–87.

Available at www.marxists.org/reference/subject/economics/jevons/mathem.htm (accessed on July 28, 2013).

Joyce, James, *A Portrait of the Artist as a Young Man.* New York: Viking, 1966.

Kandel, Eric, *In Search of Memory: The Emergence of a New Science of Mind.* New York: Norton, 2006.

Kringlebach, Morten, *The Pleasure Center: Trust Your Animal Instincts.* New York: Oxford University Press, 2008.

Kushner, Howard I., *A Cursing Brain? The Histories of Tourette Syndrome.* Cambridge: Harvard University Press, 1999.

Langevin, Helene, "The Science of Stretch: The Study of Connective Tissue and Alternative Medicine," *The Scientist,* (May 2013): 33–37.

Lewis, Bradley, *Depression: Integrating Science, Culture and Humanities.* New York: Routledge, 2012.

Livingston, William, *Pain and Suffering.* Seattle: IASP Press, 1998.

"Lobotomy." *Encyclopedia Britannica. Encyclopedia Britannica Online Academic Edition.* Encyclopedia Britannica Inc., 2013. Available at www.britannica.com.ezproxy. lib.ou.edu/EBchecked/topic/345502/lobotomy (accessed on May 26, 2013).

Mandler, G., "Consciousness: Respectable, Useful, and Probably Necessary," in *Information Processing and Cognition: The Loyola Symposium,* ed. R. Solso. Hillsdale, NJ: Lawrence Erlbaum Associates, 1975, pp. 229–54.

——, *Mind and Body: Psychology of Emotion and Stress.* New York: Norton, 1984.

Manu, Peter (ed.), *Functional Somatic Syndromes: Etiology, Diagnosis and Treatment.* New York: Cambridge University Press, 1998.

Meier, Barry, *A World of Hurt.* New York: New York Times Company, 2013. An E-book (cited with Kindle location numbers).

Melzack, Ronald, "Phantom Limbs, The Self and the Brain (The D. O. Hebb Memorial Lecture)," *Canadian Psychology/Psychologie Canadienne,* 30 (1989): 1–15.

——, "Pain: Past, Present, Future," *Canadian Journal of Experimental Psychology,* 47: 1993, 615–29.

——, "Phantom-Limb and the Brain," in *Pain and the Brain: From Nociception to Cognition,* Burkhart Bromm and John E. Desmedt (eds). *Advances in Pain Research and Therapy,* vol. 22. New York: Raven Press, 1995.

Melzack, Ronald and C. Perry, "Self-regulation of Pain: The Use of Alpha Feedback and Hypnotic Training for the Control of Pain," *Experimental Neurology,* 46 (1975): 452–69.

Melzack, Ronald and Patrick Wall, *The Challenge of Pain.* New York: Basic Books, 1983.

Minsky, M., "A Framework for Representing Knowledge," in *Mind Design,* ed. J. Haugeland. Cambridge, MA: MIT Press, 1981, pp. 95–128.

Minsky, M., *The Society of Mind.* Cambridge, MA: MIT Press, 1986.

Mithen, Steven, *The Singing Neanderthals: The Origins of Music, Language, Mind and Body.* Cambridge: Harvard University Press, 2006.

Morris, David, *The Culture of Pain.* Berkeley and Los Angeles: University of California Press, 1991.

——, *Illness and Culture in the Postmodern Age.* Berkeley and Los Angeles: University of California Press, 1998.

Moyn, Samuel, "Torture and Taboo," *The Nation*, February 25, 2013, 27–33.

Nickles, Thomas, "Kuhn, Historical Philosophy of Science, and Case-Based Reasoning," *Configurations*, 6 (1998): 51–85.

Olness, K., H. J. Wain, and N. G. Lorenz, "A Pilot Study of Blood Endorphin Levels in Children Using Self-Hypnosis to Control Pain," *Journal of Developmental and Behavioral Pediatrics*, 4 (1980): 187–88.

Ornstein, Robert, *The Right Mind: Making Sense of the Hemispheres*. New York: Harcourt, Brace, 1997.

Price, D. D. and J. J. Barrell, "Mechanisms of Analgesia Produced by Hypnosis and Placebo Suggestions," *Progress in Brain Research*, 122 (2000): 255–71.

Price D. D., J. E. Barrell, and J. J. Barrell, "A Quantitative–Experiential Analysis of Human Emotions," *Motivation and Emotion*, 9 (1985): 19–38.

Price D. D., D. G. Finniss, and F. Benedetti, "A Comprehensive Review of the Placebo Effect: Recent Advances and Current Thought," *Annual Review of Psychology*, 59 (2008): 565–90.

Price D. D., J. Riley, and J. J. Barrell, "Are Lived Choices Based on Emotional Processes?" *Cognition and Emotion*, 15 (2001): 365–79.

Ramachandran, V. S. and Sandra Blakeslee, *Phantoms in the Brain: Probing the Mysteries of the Human Mind*. New York: Quill, 1998.

Rey, Roselyne, *The History of Pain*. Trans. Louise Elliott Wallace et al. Cambridge, MA: Harvard University Press, 1993.

Robinson, Richard. *Definition*. Oxford: Oxford University Press, 1972.

Rogers, Kara, "Placebo effect." *Encyclopedia Britannica. Encyclopedia Britannica Online Academic Edition*. Encyclopedia Britannica Inc., 2013. Available at www.britannica.com.ezproxy.lib.ou.edu/EBchecked/topic/1705901/placebo-effect (accessed on May 28, 2013).

Rumelhart, David, "Schemata: The Building Blocks of Cognition," in *Theoretical Issues in Reading Comprehension*, ed. R. Spire, B. Bruce, and W. Brewer. Hillsdale, NJ: Lawrence Erlbaum Associates, 1980.

Rumelhart, David, P. Smolensky, J. L. McClelland, and G. E. Hinton, "Schemata and Sequential Thought Processes in DPD Models," in J. L. McClelland and D. E. Rumelhart, eds., *Parallel Distributed Processing: Explorations in the Microstructure of Cognition, Volume 2: Psychological and Biological Models*. Cambridge: MIT Press, 1986.

Russell, I. John, "Is Fibromyalgia a Distinct Clinical Entity? The Clinical Investigator's Evidence," *Balliere's Clinical Rheumatology*, 13 (1999): 445–54.

Saint Teresa of Avila, *The Complete Works of Saint Teresa of Jesus*, 3 vols., trans. E. Allison Peers. London: Sheed and Ward, 1946.

Scarry, Elaine, *The Body in Pain: The Making and Unmaking of the World*. New York: Oxford University Press, 1985.

Schacter, D. L., "Multiple Forms of Memory in Humans and Animals," in *Memory Systems of the Brain*, eds. N. M. Weinberger, J. L. McGaugh, and G. Lynch. New York: The Guilford Press, 1985, pp. 351–79.

Schacter, D. L. and M. Moscovitch, "Infants, Amnesics, and Dissociable Memory Systems," in *Infant Memory: In Relation to Normal and Pathological Memory in Humans and Other Animals*. New York: Plenum Press, 1984, pp. 173–216.

Schank, R. and Abelson, *Scripts, Plans, Goals, and Understanding: An Inquiry into Human Knowledge*. Hillsdale, NJ: Lawrence Erlbaum Associates, 1977.

Schleifer, Ronald, *Intangible Materialism: The Body, Scientific Knowledge, and the Power of Language*. Minneapolis: University of Minnesota Press, 2009.

——, "Modalities of Science: Phronesis, Narrative, and the Practices of Medicine," *Danish Yearbook of Philosophy*, 44 (2009a): 77–101.

——, "A new start for the humanities is required for the 21st century: a debate between Steve Fuller, Ronald Schleifer and Robert Markley," *Danish Yearbook of Philosophy*, 44 (2009b): 156–71.

——, "Narrative Knowledge, Phronesis, and Paradigm-Based Medicine," *Narrative*, 20 (2012): 64–86.

Schleifer, Ronald and Jerry Vannatta, "The Chief Concern of Medicine: Narrative, *Phronesis*, and the History of Present Illness," in *Binocular Vision: Narrative and Metaphor in Medicine*, ed. Michael Hanne, a special issue of *Genre*, 44 (2011): 335–47.

——, *The Chief Concern of Medicine: The Integration of the Medical Humanities and Narrative Knowledge into Medical Practices*. Ann Arbor: University of Michigan Press, 2013.

Showalter, Elaine, *Hystories: Hysterical Epidemics and Modern Media*. New York: Columbia University Press, 1997.

Smith, J. T., A. F. Barabasz, and M. Barabasz, "Comparison of Hypnosis and Distraction in Severely Ill Children Undergoing Painful Medical Procedures," *Journal of Counseling Psychology*, 43 (1996): 187–95.

Spiegel, D. and L. H. Albert, "Naloxone Fails to Reverse Hypnotic Alleviation of Chronic Pain," *Psychopharmacology*, 81 (1985): 140–43.

Spinhoven, P., "Similarities and Dissimilarities in Hypnotic and Nonhypnotic Procedures for Headache Control: A Review," *American Journal of Clinical Hypnosis*, 30 (1988): 183–94.

Squire, L. R., *Memory and the Brain*. New York: Oxford University Press, 1987.

Steen, Francis, "The Paradox of Narrative Thinking," *Journal of Cultural and Evolutionary Psychology*, 3 (2005): 87–105.

Steiner, William Glenn (ed.), "Drug Use." *Encyclopedia Britannica. Encyclopedia Britannica Online Academic Edition*. Encyclopedia Britannica Inc., 2013. Available at www.britannica.com.ezproxy.lib.ou.edu/EBchecked/topic/172024/drug-use (accessed on May 28, 2013).

Stevens, Janice R. and Paul H. Blachly, "Successful Treatment of the Maladie des Tics, Gilles de la Tourette's Syndrome," *American Journal of Diseases in Children*, 112 (1966): 541–45.

Thernstrom, Melanie, *The Pain Chronicles*. New York: Ferrar, Stauss, Giroux, 2010.

Thorstein Veblen, 1898. "Why Is Economics Not an Evolutionary Science?" in *Veblen on Marx, Race, Science and Economics*. New York, Capricorn Books, 1969, pp. 56–81.

Trimble, Michael R., *The Soul in the Brain: The Cerebral Basis of Language, Art, and Belief*. Baltimore: Johns Hopkins University Press, 2007.

Vannatta, Jerry, Ronald Schleifer, and Sheila Crow, *Medicine and Humanistic Understanding: The Significance of Narrative in Medical Practices*. Philadelphia: University of Pennsylvania Press, 2005. A DVD-ROM.

Vertosick, Frank, *Why We Hurt: The Natural History of Pain*. New York: Harcourt, 2000.

Wall, Patrick, *Pain: The Science of Suffering*. London: Phoenix Books, 1999.

Weil, Simone, "The Love of God and Affliction," available at payingattentiontothesky. com/2010/07/15/the-love-of-god-and-affliction-by-simone-weil, 2001 (accessed on July 1, 2013).

Weiner, Jonathan, *The Beak of the Finch*. New York: Vintage, 1995.

Wessely, Simon, C. Nimnuan, and M. Sharpe, "Functional Somatic Syndromes: One or Many?" *Lancet*, 354, 9182 (1999): 936–39.

West, B. H., "Experiments in Animal Magnetism," *Boston Medical and Surgical Journal*, 14 (1836): 349–51.

Wittgenstein, Ludwig. *Philosophical Investigations* (third edition). Trans. G.E.M. Anscombe. Oxford: Blackwell Publishing, 2001.

INDEX

Custom Materials
DELIVER A MORE REWARDING EDUCATIONAL EXPERIENCE.

University Readers
Custom Publishing Evolved

Routledge
Taylor & Francis Group

The Social Issues Collection

This unique collection features 250 readings plus 45 recently added readings for undergraduate teaching in sociology and other social science courses. The social issues collection includes selections from Joe Nevins, Sheldon Elkand-Olson, Val Jenness, Sarah Fenstermaker, Nikki Jones, France Winddance Twine, Scott McNall, Ananya Roy, Joel Best, Michael Apple, and more.

1 Go to the website at routledge.customgateway.com

2 Choose from almost 300 readings from Routledge & other publishers

3 Create your complete custom anthology

Learn more:
routledge.customgateway.com | 800.200.3908 x 501 | info@cognella.com